Place Value Through Hundred Thousands

Use the data from the table to solve Problems 1–3.

W9-BEO-180

Five Female Names	
Name	**Number of People**
Patricia	153,834
Linda	148,386
Mary	376,915
Barbara	140,500
Elizabeth	143,336

Show Your Work

1. Use the table to find the most popular of these female names. Write in word form the number of females with that name.

   Mary: three hundred seventy-six thousand, nine hundred fifteen

2. For which name(s) does the number of females have a 3 in the thousands place?

   Patricia; Elizabeth

3. Suppose 100 more females had the name Mary. How many would that be? Explain Dave's mistake. Then find the correct answer.

   377,015

4. This is the way Dave wrote the expanded form of the number of females with the name Barbara: $(140 \times 100,000) + (5 \times 100)$. Explain Dave's mistake. Then find the correct answer. Dave should have taken each digit of the number and multiplied it by its place value: $(1 \times 100,000) + (4 \times 10,000) + (5 \times 100)$.

Copyright © Houghton Mifflin Company. All rights reserved.

Use with text pages 4–5.

Name _____   Date _____

More About Place Value

Solve.

Show Your Work

1. The inventory report for a school supply warehouse shows that it has 6 pallets with 10,000 pencils each, 3 cartons with 1,000 pencils each, and 8 boxes of 100 pencils each. Write the total number of pencils they have in expanded form with exponents and in standard form.

$(6 \times 10^4) + (3 \times 10^3) + (8 \times 10^2)$; 63,800 pencils

2. A school buys a box that contains 10^4 blank CDs. If each of the 10 computer labs requested 1,000 CDs, did the school buy enough CDs for each lab to get what it wants? Explain.

Yes; Possible answer:
$10^4 = 10,000$ CDs,
and $10 \times 1,000 = 10,000$ CDs.

3. Write the exponents that make each equation true. Describe the pattern that you see.

$$4^2 = 2^\square$$
$$4^3 = 2^\square$$
$$4^4 = 2^\square$$
$$4^5 = 2^\square$$

4, 6, 8, 10; Possible answer: The exponents for numbers with a base of 2 are double the exponents of numbers with a base of 4.

4. James said that 5^4 and 4^5 represent the same number. Is James correct? Explain why or why not.

No; $5^4 = 5 \times 5 \times 5 \times 5$ or 625;
$4^5 = 4 \times 4 \times 4 \times 4 \times 4$ or 1,024.

Copyright © Houghton Mifflin Company. All rights reserved.

Use with text pages 6–7.

Name _____ Date _____

Place Value Through Hundred Billions

Use the data in the paragraph about the Sun to solve Problems 1–4.

Sun Facts

The Sun is about 4 billion 500 million years old and its expected life span is about 10 billion years. With a diameter of about 863,700 miles, the Sun is about 3×10^5 times the size of the Earth. The temperature of the Sun's core is about 27 million degrees Fahrenheit. An eruption on the Sun can cause solar winds that speed along at about 1,566,000 miles per hour. Earth is about 93,000,000 miles from the Sun.

Show Your Work

1. Is the Sun about 3 thousand, 30 thousand, 300 thousand, or 3 million times larger than Earth? Explain.

   300 thousand; 10^5 indicates the hundred thousands place; $3 \times 10^5 = 300,000$

2. Karen wrote the expected life span of the Sun as 1×10^9. Explain what she did wrong. What is the correct answer?

   $1 \times 10^9 = 1$ billion; The expected life span is 10 billion; The correct answer is 1×10^{10}.

3. Sinope is one of Jupiter's moons. Its distance from Jupiter is $(1 \times 10^7) + (4 \times 10^6) + (7 \times 10^5) + (2 \times 10^4) + (6 \times 10^3) + (5 \times 10^2)$ miles. Write this distance in word form.

   fourteen million, seven hundred twenty-six thousand, five hundred miles

4. As it orbits the Sun, Earth's speed is about $(6 \times 10,000) + (6 \times 1,000) + (7 \times 100)$. Is this greater than or less than the speed of a solar wind? Explain how you know.

   less than; Earth's orbit is about 66,700 miles per hour. Its greatest place is ten thousands, which is less than the greatest place in 1,566,000 (millions).

Copyright © Houghton Mifflin Company. All rights reserved.

Use with text pages 8–9.

Compare, Order, and Round Whole Numbers

Use the chart to solve Problems 1–4.

Internet Use in the United States in the Year 2000		
Place	**Total Population**	**Estimated Internet Users**
United States	281,422,000	116,790,130
California	33,872,000	15,818,224
Florida	15,982,000	6,904,224
Michigan	9,938,000	4,183,898
Ohio	11,353,000	4,620,671
South Carolina	4,012,000	1,283,840

Show Your Work

1. To the nearest million, how many Internet users are in the United States?

   117,000,000

2. The number of Internet users in Pennsylvania was about 4,924,681. If this data were added to the table, between which two states would its number fall?

   Ohio and Florida

3. In the United States, Alaska has the highest proportion of people on the Internet. About 348,612 of Alaska's 627,000 citizens used the Internet in 2000. Round 348,612 to the same place as the figure for the total population.

   349,000

4. New York had 7,552,448 Internet users in 2000. For which states did New York have a greater number of Internet users?

   Florida, Michigan, Ohio, South Carolina

Copyright © Houghton Mifflin Company. All rights reserved.

Use with text pages 10–12.

Place Value Through Thousandths

Solve Problems 1–4.

Show Your Work

1. Tyrant Flycatchers are among the many songbirds that live in North America. Flycatchers may weigh as little as 4.5 grams. Write this weight in word form.

four and five tenths grams

2. A sand martin makes its nest at the end of a 0.75 meter tunnel. Draw and shade a decimal square to represent 0.75.

3. A nuthatch lays 4 eggs, none of which has the same weight. If all the weights are between 1.0 and 2.0 grams, what are some possible weights for the eggs? Write your answers in standard form and in word form.

Answers will vary.

4. A thrush weighs two hundred fifteen thousandths of a kilogram. Melvin wrote the weight this way: 215,000 kilograms. How would you fix Melvin's answer?

Possible answer: Melvin wrote the whole number not the decimal two hundred fifteen thousandths. The number should be 0.215.

Copyright © Houghton Mifflin Company. All rights reserved.

Use with text pages 14–15.

Problem-Solving Strategy: Find a Pattern

1. Mr. Henry's car now has 65,000 miles on it. Its estimated value is $1,200. At 75,000 miles, the estimated value drops to $1,100. At 85,000 miles, the estimated value drops to $1,000. If the pattern continues, what will the car's estimated value be at 105,000 miles?

UNDERSTAND

What is the question?

What will the car's estimated value be at 105,000 miles?

PLAN

How can finding a pattern help you solve the problem?

Answers will vary.

Use the table to organize the data given in the problem.

Mileage	65,000	75,000	85,000
Value	$1,200	$1,100	$1,000

What patterns do you notice in the table?

Possible answer: As the miles increase by 10,000, the value decreases by $100.

SOLVE

What is the solution?

$800

LOOK BACK

How can you check your answer?

Possible answer: Check that the pattern works.

2. The Henry Company had profits of $2,010,000 the first year, $3,190,000 the second year, and $4,370,000 the third year. How much in profits would you expect the Henry Company to make in the fifth year?

$6,730,000

Copyright © Houghton Mifflin Company. All rights reserved.

Name _____ Date _____

Compare, Order, and Round Decimals

Use the data from the table to solve Problems 1–3.

2006 Middlesex County High Schools Top Five Hitters		
Player	**Team**	**Average**
Javier Ordonez	Tigers	0.320
Junior Ramirez	Griffons	0.349
Kazuya Suzuki	Eagles	0.321
Mark Sweeney	Mustangs	0.340
Tony Williams	Panthers	0.333

Show Your Work

1. In 2005, Kazuya Suzuki played his first season on the Eagles. His batting average that year was 1 thousandth less than Junior Ramirez's 2006 average. What was Kazuya Suzuki's 2005 batting average?

   _____0.348_____

2. Write the names of the players in order of greatest to least batting averages.

   Junior Ramirez, Mark Sweeney, Tony Williams, Kazuya Suzuki, Javier Ordonez

3. In 2006, the Woodland Creek High School League batting champ, Barry Worth, had an average of 0.370. Shade decimal squares to show whether the Middlesex County High School League batting leader or Barry Worth had the better average.

   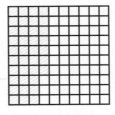 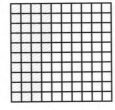

   Barry Worth

   Barry Worth had the better average.

Copyright © Houghton Mifflin Company. All rights reserved.

Use with text pages 20–22.

Expressions and Addition Properties

1. A storeowner pays x dollars for each computer game cartridge. She adds $5 to cover her expenses and y dollars for profit. Write an expression to show the final price of a game cartridge.

   $x + \$5 + y$

2. Suppose the value of x in Problem 1 is $8.95 and the value of y is $3.50. Evaluate the expression you wrote to find the price of the cartridge.

   $17.45

3. Miss Watson wrote this expression on the board: $y - 7$. One student read the expression incorrectly. Which student is it? How do you know?

   • Mary: seven less than some number
   • Tamara: some number less than 7
   • Pat: take seven from some number

   Tamara; some number less than 7 would be the expression $y < 7$, not $y - 7$.

4. Andy ordered 12 game cartridges from Company A, 15 from Company B, and 8 from Company C. He wanted to know how many games he ordered altogether. He first thought to add $(12 + 15) + 8$ but then changed his mind to $(12 + 8) + 15$. Will the sum be the same? Draw a picture to support your conclusion. Explain why he probably made the change.

   Yes; pictures and explanations will vary.

Copyright © Houghton Mifflin Company. All rights reserved.

Use with text pages 28–30.

Estimate Sums and Differences

Use the table to solve Problems 1–4.

Active Volcanoes	
Volcano	**Height (in feet)**
Kilauea, Hawaii	4,009
Mount Etna, Italy	11,053
Mount Vesuvius, Italy	4,203
Popocatépetl, Mexico	17,930
Raung, Indonesia	10,932
Soufriere Hills, Montserrat	3,001

Show Your Work

1. The tallest active volcano in the world is Llullaillaco in Chile. It is 4,127 feet taller than Popocatépetl, a volcano in Mexico. About how tall is Llullaillaco?

about 22,000 feet

2. When rounded to the nearest thousand feet, which volcanoes have about a 1,000-foot difference in height?

Soufriere Hills and either Kilauea or Mount Vesuvius

3. When Mount Vesuvius in Italy erupted in the year A.D. 79, it covered the city of Pompeii in about 60 feet of ash. About how many years ago did Mount Vesuvius erupt?

about 1,900 years ago

4. If you could stack one volcano on top of another, which volcanoes from the table would you need to stack to approximate Popocatépetl's height? Explain how you made your decision.

Possible answer: Mount Etna, Kilauea, and Soufriere Hills; explanations will vary.

Copyright © Houghton Mifflin Company. All rights reserved.

Use with text pages 32–33.

Name _____ Date _____

Add and Subtract Whole Numbers

You can join a bicycle tour across the United States.
Use the map to solve Problems 1–4.

Bike Tour Across the United States

Show Your Work

1. How far do people bike during the first
two weeks on the tour? How much more
or less than that do they travel during
the next two weeks?

   1,039 miles; 82 miles
   less than Week 1

2. How much farther do the bicyclists
travel during Week 3 than Week 4?
Draw a model to show how you know.

   57 mi

Week 3 Miles: 507	
Week 4 Miles: 450	Difference: 57

3. You sign up for two consecutive weeks.
You bike 22 miles less than 1,000 miles.
Which two weeks of the tour did you
ride? Explain how you decided.

   Weeks 2 and 3; 1,000 − 22 = 978.
   Explanations will vary.

4. You want to find the total number of
miles covered by this cross-country bike
tour. Explain how you will organize the
data and solve the problem. Then solve
the problem. Show your work.

   Possible answer: Add the first two weeks
   and then one more week to each sum in
   turn. Total miles is 4,194.

Copyright © Houghton Mifflin Company. All rights reserved.

Use with text pages 34–36.

Add and Subtract Greater Numbers

Companies pay millions of dollars to show their ads on
TV during the Super Bowl. Use the data in the table
to solve Problems 1–4.

Super Bowl Advertising		
Year	Price for a 30-second ad	Number of TV Viewers
1997	$1,200,000	87,870,000
1998	$1,300,000	90,000,000
1999	$1,600,000	83,720,000
2000	$2,100,000	88,465,000
2001	$2,050,000	84,335,000
2002	$1,900,000	87,000,000

Show Your Work

1. In 1967, the first year of the Super
Bowl, one 30-second commercial cost
$42,000. By how much had the cost
increased by the year 2000?

   $2,058,000

2. In 2002, one company bought the
equivalent of six 30-second commercials.
Did they spend more or less than one
billion dollars? Explain how you know.

   Less than $1 billion;
   when you add $1,900,000
   six times you get
   $11,400,000 which is
   much less than $1 billion.

3. In 2002, the Super Bowl was played in a
sold-out stadium. The stadium's capacity
is 76,791. How many more people
watched the game at home than in the
stadium?

   86,923,209 people

4. Between which two consecutive years
did the number of people watching the
Super Bowl on television change the
least? Describe the change and the way
you figured it out.

   1997–1998; explanations will vary.

Copyright © Houghton Mifflin Company. All rights reserved.

Use with text pages 38–39.

Addition and Subtraction Equations

Show Your Work

1. Chen has 20 rows in his garden. He plants 6 rows of broccoli and he plants carrots in the rest of the rows. How many rows of carrots did Chen plant? Draw a model and write an equation to represent the problem.

   $6 + n = 20$

Total Rows: 20	
rows of broccoli: 6	rows of carrots: n

2. Bobby needs to find the number of bushels of apples he sold out of the 50 bushels he started with. He has 16 bushels left to sell. He wrote this equation: $n - 50 = 16$.

   What did Bobby do wrong? What should the equation be? How many bushels did he sell?

   He subtracted the total amount from the part he sold. The equation should be $50 - n = 16$; $n = 34$ bushels

3. You decide what the following equation represents.

   $$\$10 - n = \$4.50$$

   Write a problem to fit the equation. Solve your problem.

   Answers will vary.

Copyright © Houghton Mifflin Company. All rights reserved.

Use with text pages 40–41.

Problem-Solving Decision:
Relevant Information

Problem The library has 2,000 books for sale. The books are sorted into nonfiction, fiction, and children's books. The children's books number 500. There are 200 more fiction books than nonfiction books. How many fiction books and nonfiction books are for sale in all?

UNDERSTAND

What is the question?

How many fiction and nonfiction books are for sale in all?

PLAN

What information helps you to solve the problem?

2,000 books; 500 children's books

What information do you **not** need to know?

200 more fiction books than nonfiction books

SOLVE

Draw a model to solve the problem.

Total number of books: 2,000	
Number of children's books: 500	Number of fiction and nonfiction books: n

Use the model to write an equation.

$2,000 = 500 + n$

Solve the equation.

$2,000 - 500 = 1,500; n = 1,500$

Answer the question.

There are 1,500 fiction and nonfiction books for sale.

LOOK BACK

How do you know that you answered the question?

Subtracting the number of children's books from the total left all the rest of the books, which are the fiction and nonfiction books.

Copyright © Houghton Mifflin Company. All rights reserved.

Use with text pages 42–43.

Expressions and Multiplication Properties

The chart shows the jobs middle school students do as part of a fundraiser. Use the information to solve Problems 1–4.

Jobs We Will Do For You!	
Job	**Price**
Babysitting	$2 per hour per child
Car Washing	$5 per car
Yard Work	$6 per hour
Attic Cleaning	$4 per hour
Errand Running	$3 per hour

Show Your Work

1. Mr. Green hires Brianna to do yard work for n hours. Write an expression to find the amount Brianna will charge for the work. Then use the expression to find the amount Brianna will charge for 4 hours of yard work.

   $6n$; $24

2. In the first hour, Percy washed r cars. In the next hour, he washed 4 cars. Write two expressions to show how much he earned each hour. If Percy washed 5 cars in the first hour, find how much he earned in all.

   $5r$; 5×4; $45

3. Use the expression $4 \times n$ to show the cost for attic cleaning. Belle worked 7 hours. Curtis worked 23 hours. Write an expression to show how much money each raised by working. Then solve.

   Belle: 4×7, Curtis: 4×23; Belle: $28, Curtis: $92

4. Amy wants to figure out how much she will earn. She uses the expression $3n$ to find the total amount. Explain how you can tell which job she will do. Suppose she works 12 hours. How can you figure out how much she will earn? Explain your thinking.

   Running errands is the only job that pays $3 per hour. $12 \times 3 = $36; the number of hours (12) times fee per hour ($3) is $36.

Copyright © Houghton Mifflin Company. All rights reserved.

Use with text pages 60–61.

Name _____   Date _____

Model the Distributive Property

**Shade and divide a grid to model the solutions for each of
Problems 1–3. Use the Distributive Property to find each product.**

1–4: Check models.   **Show Your Work**

1. A marching band has 24 rows with
8 marchers in each row. How many
marchers are there in all?

192 marchers

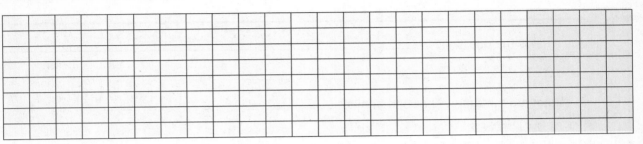

2. Six bands each have 18 baton twirlers.
How many baton twirlers are there in all?

108 baton twirlers

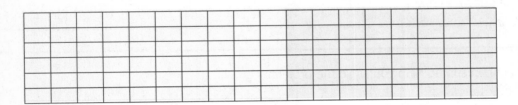

3. Four members from each of 15 marching
bands will participate in a special
performance. How many band members
will participate in all?

60 band members

4. The three best bands each have
36 marchers. Each member receives
a ribbon. Use the Distributive Property
to explain how to figure out how many
ribbons are needed. Then solve.

Possible answer:
Find (3 × 30) + (3 × 6);
108 ribbons

Copyright © Houghton Mifflin Company. All rights reserved.

Use with text pages 62–63.

Problem-Solving Strategy: Use Logical Reasoning

Problem For lunch, Emma, Rosa, and Vanya each bring a sandwich (a tuna roll, a turkey wrap, or a veggie wrap) and a drink (water, milk, or apple juice). Both Rosa and Emma bring wraps. Vanya does not drink juice. Emma does not eat fish or meat and is allergic to apple juice. The person who brings tuna doesn't bring water. What does each person bring for lunch?

UNDERSTAND

What is the question? _How does each person bring for lunch?_

What are the sandwiches and drinks? _tuna roll, turkey wrap, veggie wrap, water, milk, juice_

What do you know about: **a.** Emma? _wrap; no fish; no meat; no juice_

b. Rosa? _wrap_   **c.** Vanya? _no juice_

What other fact do you know? _One brings tuna and no water._

PLAN

How can logical reasoning help you solve the problem?

Make a table with the clues you know.

SOLVE

Fill in the table with person's name, sandwich, and drink.
Then write *yes* or *no*.

	Sandwich			Drink		
Name	t.r.	t.w.	v.w.	wat.	milk	juice
Emma	no	no	yes	yes	no	no
Rosa	no	yes	no	no	no	yes
Vanya	yes	no	no	no	yes	no

What is the solution? _Emma: veggie wrap, water; Rosa: turkey wrap, juice; Vanya: tuna roll, milk._

LOOK BACK

How did the table help you to solve the problem?

Eliminate choices.

Copyright © Houghton Mifflin Company. All rights reserved.

Use with text pages 64–66.

Multiply by One-Digit Numbers

Show Your Work

1. In one school, there are 6 fifth-grade classes with 28 students in each class. How many fifth-graders are in the school? Explain how to use the Distributive Property to find the answer.

   168; (6 × 20) + (6 × 8) = 120 + 48 = 168

2. Each morning 8 buses bring students to the school. If each bus holds an average of 45 students, how many students arrive by bus each day?

   360 students

3. Students in District A go to school 5 days a week for 44 weeks a year, 5 hours each day. Students in District B go to school 180 days for 7 hours each day. How many more or fewer hours are the students in District A in school than the students in District B?

   160 fewer hours

4. For a district art show, 382 classes each donated 4 paintings. Anna found the total number of paintings this way.

   $$\begin{array}{r} 382 \\ \times\ \ \ 4 \\ \hline 12,328 \end{array}$$

   Explain what she did wrong and what the correct answer is.

   Possible answer: When she multiplied 4 × 80, she did not regroup the 32 tens as 3 hundreds 2 tens; 1,528.

Copyright © Houghton Mifflin Company. All rights reserved.

Use with text pages 68–70.

Patterns in Multiples of 10

Show Your Work

1. The post office sells books of 20 stamps
and rolls of 100 stamps. If a customer
buys 5 books of stamps and 4 rolls of
stamps, how many stamps does the
customer buy altogether?

   500 stamps

2. Paper hinges attach stamps to albums. A
stamp dealer has 20 packages of hinges
with 1,000 hinges per package. If she
sells all but 9 packages, how many
hinges does she sell?

   11,000 hinges

3. A sheet of one-cent stamps is set in an
array of 5 stamps × 10 stamps. How
many stamps are on 300 sheets?

   15,000 stamps

4. Stamp collectors put their extra stamps in
special envelopes. You can buy a small
pack of 100 envelopes for $3 per pack or
a large pack of 1,000 envelopes for $20
per pack. Decide how many small and
large packs a stamp collector will buy and
find the total price.

   Answers will vary.

5. A stamp dealer sells packages of assorted
stamps. There are 200, 300, 400, 600, or
800 stamps in a package. A customer
buys 3 of the same package and gets a
total of 2,400 stamps. Which set of stamps
did the customer buy? Explain how you
can use a pattern to check your work.

   800 stamps per pack-
   age; use the pattern:
   3 × 8 = 24
   3 × 80 = 240
   3 × 800 = 2,400

Copyright © Houghton Mifflin Company. All rights reserved.

Estimate Products

Use the data from the table to solve Problems 1–4.

Sports Drink	
Container	**Fluid Ounces**
Small bottle	16
Medium bottle	32
Large bottle	64
Powder Packet	320 (when mixed with water)

Show Your Work

1–4: Estimates may vary.

1. A family buys 2 cases of the small bottles of sports drink. If there are 24 bottles per case, about how many ounces of sports drink did the family buy?

   about 800 fluid ounces

2. Suppose another family buys 2 cases of the large bottles. If there are 8 large bottles in each case, does the family buy the same, more, or fewer ounces of sports drink than the family in Problem 1? Explain.

   More. The family in Problem 2 buys about 900 fluid ounces, which is more than the family in Problem 1.

3. A box of sports drink has 12 rows of bottles and 24 bottles in each row. Each row is 8 bottles deep. A clerk estimates the total number of bottles:

   $(12 \times 24) \times 8 \approx (10 \times 30) \times 10$
   $300 \times 10 = 3,000$ bottles

   What did he do wrong?

   He rounded up instead of down. The answer is $(12 \times 24) \times 8 \approx (10 \times 20) \times 10 = 200 \times 10 = 2,000$ bottles.

4. A store owner orders 180 cases of small bottles and 85 cases of medium bottles of sports drink. If there are 24 small bottles per case and 12 medium bottles per case, about how many bottles are there in all? Explain how you found your answer.

   Possible answer: about 4,900 bottles; estimate small bottles ($180 \times 24 \approx 200 \times 20 = 4,000$), and medium bottles ($85 \times 12 \approx 90 \times 10 = 900$); add the estimates.

Copyright © Houghton Mifflin Company. All rights reserved.

Use with text pages 74–75.

Multiply by Two-Digit Numbers

Use the data in the table to solve Problems 1–4.

Time Equivalents

60 seconds = 1 minute

60 minutes = 1 hour

24 hours = 1 day

7 days = 1 week

52 weeks = 1 year

12 months = 1 year

365 days = 1 year

Show Your Work

1. An average fifth-grader is 11 years old. How many months is that?

_____ 132 months _____

2. Suppose that Problem 1 had asked for the average age of a fifth-grader in weeks. What would the answer be then?

_____ 572 weeks _____

3. How many seconds are in one day? Explain how you found your answer.

86,400 seconds; 60 × 60 = 3,600 (the number of seconds in one hour) and 3,600 × 24 = 86,400 (the number of seconds in 24 hours, or one day)

4. Sharon's mother is 45 years old. Sharon figured out her age in days this way.

```
    2 2
    3 2
    3 6 5
  ×   4 5
  1 8 2 5
+ 1 4 6 0
  3, 2 8 5 days
```

Explain what Sharon did wrong and how to find the correct answer.

_____

She did not add a placeholder space or zero.

```
    2 2
    3 2
    3 6 5
  ×   4 5
  1 8 2 5
+ 1 4 6 0 0
  1 6, 4 2 5 days
```

Copyright © Houghton Mifflin Company. All rights reserved.

Problem-Solving Decision: Explain Your Solution

Problem The teachers at West Elementary School are planning a field trip for 385 students. It will cost $1,750 for transportation and $3,080 for tickets to the museum. If the teachers charge each student $12, will they have enough money to cover the costs of the field trip?

UNDERSTAND

What is the question?
Will $12 be enough money?

How many students are going on the field trip?
385 students

What is the cost for:

a. transportation? $1,750

b. museum tickets? $3,080

How much do the teachers plan to charge each student?
$12

PLAN

How could estimating help solve the problem?
If your estimate answers the question, you don't have to find the exact answer.

SOLVE

Find the total cost of the trip.
$4,830

Did you solve the problem? If not, find an exact answer.
No; $12 × 385 = $4,620

Estimate the amount of money the teachers will collect from the students.
Possible answer: 10 × 400 = $4,000; 20 × 400 = $8,000

What is the solution?
$12 is not enough.

LOOK BACK

Explain why your solution needed to be exact or why an estimate was sufficient.
Estimating range was too great; $12 is much closer to $10 than $20.

Copyright © Houghton Mifflin Company. All rights reserved.

Use with text pages 80–81.

Name _____ Date _____

Estimate Quotients

Use the data from the chart to solve Problems 1–4.

				Mileage Between Cities				
Cities	Detroit/ Chicago	Detroit/ Cleveland	Detroit/ Des Moines	Detroit/ Houston	Detroit/ Louisville	Chicago/ Cleveland	Cleveland/ Des Moines	Louisville/ Chicago
Miles	266	170	584	1,265	360	335	652	292

Show Your Work

1–4: *Possible answers are given.*

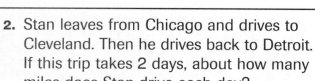

1. Stan is a trucker who lives in Detroit. It takes him about 5 hours to go from Detroit to Chicago. On average, about how many miles does he travel each hour? Draw base ten blocks to check your work.

   about 50 miles
   _____

2. Stan leaves from Chicago and drives to Cleveland. Then he drives back to Detroit. If this trip takes 2 days, about how many miles does Stan drive each day?

   about 250 miles
   _____

3. Suppose instead of going to Detroit from Cleveland Stan first drives to Des Moines. If he covers the Chicago-Cleveland-Des Moines-Detroit trip in 3 days, about how far does he travel each day?

   about 500 miles
   _____

4. Use the data in the chart to plan a trip for Stan that goes to at least three cities. Decide on a reasonable number of days for him to make the trip. Then show how many miles he covers each day.

   Answers will vary.
   _____

Copyright © Houghton Mifflin Company. All rights reserved.

Use with text pages 86–87.

One-Digit Divisors

Solve Problems 1–5.

Show Your Work

1. Emilio wants to buy a bike for $189. He saves $9 each week from his paper route. How many weeks will he need to save the money for the bike?

   _____21 weeks_____

2. Maggie earns $96 each week bagging groceries at the store. She saves half of her earnings each week. How much money does she save each week?

   _____$48_____

3. Otis' parents saved $345 in 3 months for a vacation. If they continue to save the same amount each month, how much will they save in 5 months?

   _____$575_____

4. Robert, Mike, and Corey each saved $264 for basketball camp. Robert saved his money in 8 weeks. Mike saved his money 2 weeks faster than Robert. Corey saved his money in half the time that Robert did. How much did each boy save each week?

   Robert: $33; Mike: $44; Corey: $66

5. Janet is saving for a car that costs $4,596. She did this division to find how much she has to save each year for 3 years to pay for the car. Explain what Janet did wrong.

   _____

$$\begin{array}{r} \$153 \\ 3\overline{)\$4,596} \\ -3 \\ \hline 15 \\ -15 \\ \hline 09 \\ -9 \\ \hline 0 \end{array}$$

   She did not divide the ones. The answer should be $1,532.

Copyright © Houghton Mifflin Company. All rights reserved.

Use with text pages 88–89.

Problem-Solving Application:
Use Operations

Problem You are thinking about getting all guppies, all neon tetras, or all goldfish for your aquarium. The total length of all the fish in the tank should not be greater than the number of gallons the tank holds. What is the greatest number of each kind of fish you could have in a 20-gallon tank? In a 55-gallon tank?

Freshwater Aquarium Fish	
Fish	**Size (in inches)**
Guppy	2
Neon tetra	1
Goldfish	4

UNDERSTAND

What is the question? What is the greatest number of each kind of fish in a 20-gallon tank and a 55-gallon tank?

What do you know about the total length of all the fish? Inches in length of the fish should not be greater than the number of gallons the tank holds.

How many inches long is each:

guppy? 2

neon tetra? 1

goldfish? 4

PLAN

How can you find the greatest number of each fish for each tank? Divide the gallons each tank holds by the length of each type of fish in inches.

SOLVE

Find the number of each fish you can have in a 20-gallon tank.

10 guppies; 20 neon tetras; 5 goldfish

Find the number of each fish you can have in a 55-gallon tank.

27 guppies; 55 neon tetras; 13 goldfish

LOOK BACK

How can you check your answers? Multiply the fish by the number of inches in length.

Copyright © Houghton Mifflin Company. All rights reserved.

Use with text pages 90–91.

Name _____   Date _____

Divisibility

Use the data from the table to solve Problems 1–4.

Extended-Day Program					
Activity	Basketball	Board games	Computer games	Kickball	Street hockey
Number of Players	5 per team	4 per game	2 per computer	9 per team	6 per team

Show Your Work

1. One day 145 students played the same team sport. Which team sport was it? Explain how you used divisibility rules to decide.

   Basketball; numbers that have a 5 in the ones place are divisible by 5; the other divisibility rules do not work for 145.

2. Suppose instead of 145 students who played the same team sport, 138 students played. Would the sport they all played stay the same? If not, tell which sport it would be. How did you decide?

   No; street hockey because 138 is divisible by 6 (138 is divisible by 2 and 3).

3. On a rainy day, Mr. Ahearn told 138 students that they could all play board games. How can you use divisibility rules to show that Mr. Ahearn was wrong?

   Board games require 4 players, but 138 is not divisible by 4 because the last two digits, 38, are not divisible by 4.

4. Between 100 and 300 students are involved in the program. Decide how many students will attend on one day. Choose a number for which there are at least 3 activities all the students can participate in. Name the activities.

   Answers will vary.

Copyright © Houghton Mifflin Company. All rights reserved.

Use with text pages 92–94.

Zeros in the Quotient

Solve Problems 1–4.

Show Your Work

1. Alex ran 208 kilometers last month.
What was the average number of
kilometers he ran each week?

_____ 52 _____

2. Sarina jogged 403 kilometers in 2 months.
What was the average number of
kilometers she jogged each month?

_____ 201 _____

3. Deena runs 112,654 meters every week.
Raul said that she runs a little more than
16,007 meters each day. What is wrong
with Raul's answer? What should the
correct answer be?

Instead of finding how
many times 7 goes into
65, Raul put an extra 0

_____
in the quotient and found how many times 7
goes into 54 instead; 16,093

4. Khalid jogs 8 kilometers every day. He
wants to jog at least 3,000 kilometers by
the end of one year. At his current rate,
will he be able to reach his goal? If not,
how many miles should he jog every
day to reach his goal? Explain how
you decided.

No; at least 9 kilometers; $3,000 \div 8 = 375$,
which is more days than there are in a year
and $3,000 \div 9 = 333$ R3, which is fewer days
than there are in a year.

Copyright © Houghton Mifflin Company. All rights reserved.

Use with text pages 96–97.

Problem-Solving Strategy:
Guess and Check

Problem Lucas has 18 coins—pennies, nickels, and dimes—in his pocket. There are three times as many pennies as dimes and twice as many nickels as dimes. The number of each coin is divisible by 3, and the number of nickels is also divisible by 2. How many of each coin does Lucas have?

UNDERSTAND

What do you know?

Lucas has 18 coins.

PLAN

How can the guess-and-check strategy help you solve the problem?

Guess different combinations of coins that total 18 and then check to see if they fit the other facts of the problem.

SOLVE

Fill in the table with your first guess. Check your answer. Do you need another guess? Why or why not?

Answers will vary.

18 coins		
___ pennies	___ nickels	___ dimes

Fill in the table with your second guess. Check your answer. Do you need another guess? Why or why not?

Answers will vary.

18 coins		
___ pennies	___ nickels	___ dimes

What is the solution?

Lucas has 9 pennies, 6 nickels, and 3 dimes.

LOOK BACK

How do you know that your answer is reasonable? There are 18 coins in all, and they fit all the other facts in the problem.

Copyright © Houghton Mifflin Company. All rights reserved.

Use with text pages 98–100.

Solve Equations

Solve Problems 1–5.

Show Your Work

1. Mr. Nelson brought 36 cupcakes for the bake sale. He put the same number of cupcakes on each of 9 plates. Draw a model to show how many cupcakes were on each plate. Then solve the equation.

   $n = 4$ cupcakes

   $36 \div n = 9$

36								
n	n	n	n	n	n	n	n	n

2. Before the school bake sale started, Ms. Wilson put a cash box at each of the 8 tables. If she left $40 in all, how much did she leave in each cash box? Write an equation. Then solve.

   $40 \div n = 8$; $n = 5$; she left $5 in each box.

3. Each pie at the bake sale cost $3. The school earned $24 on the sale of pies. How many pies were sold in all? Write an equation. Then solve.

   $3n = 24$; $n = 8$; there were 8 pies in all.

4. Meg's mother baked 4 dozen cookies and put them into bags. She put 6 cookies in each bag. How many bags did she fill? Write an equation. Then solve.

   $6n = 48$; 8 bags

5. Decide what the variables y and n represent in the equation $y = 5n$. Then write a problem that matches your equation. Solve your problem.

   Answers will vary.

Copyright © Houghton Mifflin Company. All rights reserved.

Use with text pages 102–104.

Divide by Multiples of 10, 100, and 1,000

Show Your Work

1. Fort Bowie National Historic Site in Arizona covers 1,000 acres. The Abraham Lincoln Boyhood National Memorial in Indiana covers 200 acres. How many times larger is Fort Bowie National Historic Site than the Abraham Lincoln Boyhood National Memorial?

_____ 5 times _____

2. The Tuskegee Airmen National Historic Site is located on 90 acres. American Samoa National Park in American Samoa covers 9,000 acres. How many times larger is American Samoa National Park than the Tuskegee Airmen National Historic Site?

_____ 100 times _____

3. Alaska is about 1,500 miles long. This is about 50 times the width of Rhode Island. About how many miles wide is Rhode Island?

_____ about 30 miles _____

4. Without dividing, explain how can you tell that 63,000 ÷ 700 will have the same quotient as 630 ÷ 7?

Possible answer: use a division pattern. If you take two zeros away from each side of 63,000 ÷ 700, you get 630 ÷ 7.

Copyright © Houghton Mifflin Company. All rights reserved.

Use with text pages 110–111.

Two-Digit Divisors

Show Your Work

1. Jeff collects calendars. On his last trip to buy calendars he had $65. If the calendars he wanted cost $12 each, how many calendars could he buy?

_____5 calendars_____

2. Darla's father baked cookies for her class. He made 82 cookies. There are 23 students and 1 teacher in the class. How many cookies could each person have? How many were left?

_____3 cookies;_____
10 cookies left over

3. In the last 2 weeks, Michael received 240 new e-mails. On average, how many e-mails did he receive each day?

about 17 e-mails

4. Tameka divided 363 by 58 and answered 6. Explain what Tameka's mistake was. Then tell the correct answer.

Tameka forgot the
remainder of 15;
the answer should be 6 R15.

Copyright © Houghton Mifflin Company. All rights reserved.

Use with text pages 112–113.

Problem-Solving Strategy:
Work Backward

Problem George Washington was the first president of the United States. If you were to subtract 87 from the year Washington's term ended and then divide by 30, you will find how old Washington was when he became president. Washington was also the president of the Constitutional Convention, which occurred in 1787, 10 years before his term as U.S. president ended. How old was Washington when he became president of the U.S.?

UNDERSTAND

What is the question? How old was he when he became president?

When was the Constitutional Convention? in 1787

What other facts do you know? 3. Convention was 10 years before Washington's term ended. Subtract 87 from term end, divide by 30, to find Washington's age.

PLAN

How can you work backward to solve the problem? Start with 1787, add 10, then subtract 87, and, finally, divide by 30.

SOLVE

When did Washington's term end? 1797

Subtract 87 from the year his term ended and then divide that number by 30. 57

What is the solution? Washington was 57.

LOOK BACK

How do you know your answer is reasonable? 57 seems like a reasonable age.

Copyright © Houghton Mifflin Company. All rights reserved.

Use with text pages 114–116.

Adjusting Quotients

Show Your Work

1. The average person in Denmark eats about 283 ounces of candy each year. There are 16 ounces in one pound. About how many pounds of candy does the average person in Denmark eat each year?

<u>   about 18 pounds   </u>

2. The average Swiss eats 352 ounces of chocolate yearly. Which estimated numbers could you use to find about how many ounces of chocolate are eaten each week? Find about how many ounces of chocolate are eaten each week.

<u>   350 ÷ 50; 7 ounces   </u>

3. It takes the average American two years to eat as much chocolate as the average Swiss eats in one year. About how many ounces of chocolate does an average American eat each month?

<u>   about 15 ounces   </u>

4. Marisa said that the Swiss eat about 30 ounces of chocolate each month. Is she correct? Explain.

<u>Marisa is correct.</u>
<u>352 ÷ 12 is 29 R4,</u>
<u>which is about 30.</u>

Copyright © Houghton Mifflin Company. All rights reserved.

Use with text pages 118–119.

Division With Greater Numbers

Show Your Work

1. A group of students are walking from
    Denver to New York City, a distance of
    1,771 miles. If they walk 24 miles each
    day, how many days will the trip take?

    between 73 and 74 days

2. Another group is cycling from Los
    Angeles to Boston, a distance of 2,979
    miles. The group plans to complete the
    trip in 45 days. How many miles does
    the group need to cycle each day?

    between 66 and 67 miles

3. The distance between San Francisco and
    Cape Town, South Africa, is 10,248 miles.
    If an airplane flies 500 miles per hour,
    about how many hours would it take to
    fly from San Francisco to Cape Town?

    about 20 hours

4. How can you check an answer of a
    quotient with a remainder? Use quotient,
    dividend, and divisor in your answer.

    First multiply the quotient
    by the divisor. Then add the
    remainder to get the dividend.

Copyright © Houghton Mifflin Company. All rights reserved.

Use with text pages 120–122.

Order of Operations

Show Your Work

1. Rewrite the following expression so that the answer is 45. Add parentheses where needed. $7 \times 4 + 3 - 2^2$

   $\underline{7 \times (4 + 3) - 2^2}$

2. Look at the expression in Problem 1. Simplify the expression without the parentheses.

   $\underline{27}$

3. Rewrite the following expression so that the answer is 40. Add parentheses where needed. $8 \div 2 + 9 \times 7 - 3$

   $\underline{8 \div 2 + 9 \times (7 - 3)}$

4. Explain how to use only the number 5 and the order of operations to write an expression that equals 49. Include the expression.

   $\underline{\text{Possible answer: } 5 \times (5 + 5) - (5 \div 5)}$

5. Write a problem that involves the order of operations. Use at least three operations. List the order of operations that you are using. Then solve the problem.

   $\underline{\text{Answers will vary.}}$

Copyright © Houghton Mifflin Company. All rights reserved.

Use with text pages 124–126.

Problem-Solving Application:
Interpret Remainders

Problem The community center is offering a bus trip to a WNBA game. If each bus holds 46 passengers and 195 people sign up for the trip, how many buses will be needed?

UNDERSTAND

What is the question?

How many buses will be needed for the trip?

How many people does each bus hold?

46

How many people can sign up for the trip?

195

PLAN

How should you interpret the remainder?

If there is a remainder, increase the quotient.

SOLVE

Write and solve the division problem.

$195 \div 46 = 4 \text{ R}11$

What is the solution?

5 buses are needed

LOOK BACK

How can you check your answer?

$5 \times 46 = 230$, which is greater than the number of possible passengers.

Copyright © Houghton Mifflin Company. All rights reserved.

Use with text pages 128–130.

Measurement Concepts

Show Your Work

1. Ms. Jackson wants to know the distance between New Orleans and Miami. Is a precise measurement needed or is an estimate sufficient? Explain.

   Estimate; *Possible answer:* Knowing the approximate mileage is sufficient.

2. Mr. Grant wants to find the length and width of a doorframe so that he can install a new door. Is a precise measurement needed or is an estimate sufficient? Explain.

   precise measurement; *Possible answer:* A door measurement even slightly too large or too small could affect the door's fit in the frame.

3. Suppose you are looking at an object under a microscope. Would you want to estimate to the nearest centimeter or to a smaller unit of measure? Explain.

   a smaller unit of measure; *Possible answer:* A microscope magnifies very small objects and an estimate to the nearest centimeter will almost always be zero.

4. You want to find the height of your school building. Do you need to know the height to the nearest quarter inch? Explain.

   No; *Possible answer:* Knowing the number of feet in the height is sufficient.

Copyright © Houghton Mifflin Company. All rights reserved.

Use with text pages 148–149.

Name _____ Date _____

Customary Units of Length

Show Your Work

1. In basketball, the free-throw line is
   15 feet from the basket. How many
   inches is it?

   __180 inches__

2. Each base in baseball is 90 feet from the
   next base. How many yards is that?

   __30 yards__

3. Which customary unit or units of
   measure would you use to measure
   a classmate's height?

   Possible answer: feet and inches

4. The distance from goal post to goal post
   on a football field is 120 yards. How
   many feet is that?

   __360 feet__

5. Robert Pershing Wadlow, the tallest man
   to have ever been measured, was 8 feet
   11 inches tall. What is his height in
   inches? Why do you think a person's
   height is often written using both feet
   and inches?

   107 inches; _Possible
   answer:_ It is easier for
   me to visualize 8 feet
   11 inches than 107 inches. This could
   be one reason why both feet and inches are
   used to describe a person's height.

Copyright © Houghton Mifflin Company. All rights reserved.

Use with text pages 150–151.

Customary Units of Weight and Capacity

Show Your Work

1. The blue whale is the largest creature on Earth. A blue whale can weigh as much as 286,000 pounds. How many tons is that?

_____143 tons_____

2. The hawksbill turtle weighs 2,400 ounces. Does it weigh more or less than a 200-pound man?

_____less_____

3. Edie's mother asked her to buy a gallon of milk on her way home from school. Edie came home with 8 pints. Is this the same amount? Explain.

Yes; 8 pt = 4 qt and 4 qt = 1 gal

4. Doctors recommend drinking 8 cups of water each day. How many quarts is that?

_____2 quarts_____

5. When Ryan's baby sister was born, she weighed 6 pounds 8 ounces. Ryan said his sister weighed 80 ounces. What was Ryan's mistake? How many ounces did his sister weigh?

Possible answer: Ryan converted pounds to ounces by multiplying by 12, not 16; 104 ounces

Copyright © Houghton Mifflin Company. All rights reserved.

Use with text pages 152–154.

Name _____ Date _____

Metric Units of Length

Show Your Work

1. Would you describe the distance
   between San Diego, California, and
   Fargo, North Dakota, in terms of meters
   or kilometers? Explain.
   kilometers; A more precise measurement is unnecessary.

2. Roscoe said a meter stick measures
   100 millimeters. What is Roscoe's mistake?
   Roscoe forgot a 0 because: 1,000 mm = 1 m.

3. During a holiday show, the prop department wanted to know whether to make
   a banner 2 centimeters long or 2 meters
   long. Which measurement should the
   prop department use?
   2 meters

4. The longest Olympic race measured in
   metric units is the 10,000-meter run.
   What other metric measure could be
   used to name that race?
   Possible answer: 10 kilometer

5. Would you describe the distance from
   Boston to Seattle in centimeters? Would
   you describe the length of your textbook
   in kilometers? Why are the different
   units of measurement helpful?
   No; No; Possible answer: The different units allow you to give a more precise measurement.

Copyright © Houghton Mifflin Company. All rights reserved.

Use with text pages 156–159.

Metric Units of Mass and Capacity

Show Your Work

1. Susie drank 4 units of water in one day.
   Which unit is she more likely to drink:
   1 milliliter, 1 deciliter, or 1 liter? Explain.

   1 liter; Possible answer: one milliliter is barely a drop and 1 deciliter is less than a small glass.

2. Fat in food is measured in grams. If Bob
   eats 50 fat grams each day, how many
   milligrams of fat does he eat daily?

   50,000 milligrams

3. Which of the following amounts of dog
   food are you most likely to buy for a
   large dog, 15 grams or 15 kilograms?
   Explain.

   15 kilograms; Possible answer: 15 grams is a small amount of food, about the size of $\frac{1}{2}$ bowl of cereal.

4. A punch bowl holds 80 deciliters of
   punch. How many liters is that?

   8 liters

5. One milliliter of water weighs one gram.
   Explain the relationship between the
   conversion. Then, draw a conversion
   chart to show the relationship between
   one milliliter of water and grams,
   milligrams, kilograms, and metric tons.

   Possible answer: The conversion shows one milliliter of water would weigh 1 gram. Charts will vary.

Copyright © Houghton Mifflin Company. All rights reserved.

Use with text pages 160–162.

Add and Subtract Measurements

Show Your Work

1. A cooler was filled with a gallon of water. Tammy drank a cup. How much water was left? Use quarts, pints, and cups in your answer.

   3 quarts 1 pint 1 cup

2. Jackie ordered 1 pound 12 ounces of cheese and 2 pounds 4 ounces of ham. What is the total weight of the items that Jackie ordered?

   4 pounds

3. Ming is balancing a scale. On the left side, there are two objects. One has a mass of 150 milligrams, the other has a mass of 3 grams. On the right side, there is one object with a mass of 2,500 milligrams. What mass in milligrams does Ming need to add to the right side to balance the scale?

   650 milligrams

4. Two of the tallest players in NBA history were 7 feet 7 inches tall. The shortest player in NBA history was 5 feet 3 inches tall. How many inches shorter was the shortest player than one of the tallest players?

   28 inches

5. You are an architect examining the blueprints for a building. You notice that all the measurements are off by an inch. Explain how this might affect your building.

   Possible answer: If all measurements are an inch smaller, building will work. If some measurements are an inch greater and some are an inch less, building won't work.

Copyright © Houghton Mifflin Company. All rights reserved.

Use with text pages 164–165.

Problem-Solving Decision:
Multistep Problems

Show Your Work

1. The train from Point Pleasant leaves
   at 5:47 and arrives in Long Branch
   33 minutes later. After waiting at the
   Long Branch station for 14 minutes, the
   train leaves for New York. The trip from
   Long Branch to New York takes 1 hour
   20 minutes. What time does the train
   arrive in New York?

   7:54

2. Samuel takes the train from Point
   Pleasant to New York. It takes him about
   15 minutes to bike from his house to
   Point Pleasant. About how long does it
   take Samuel to get from his house to
   New York?

   2 hours 22 minutes

3. Maddy takes the train from Point
   Pleasant to Long Branch. She needs
   12 minutes to walk from her apartment
   to the Point Pleasant train station and
   12 minutes to walk from the Long
   Branch train station to her office. How
   long does it take Maddy to get from
   her apartment to her office?

   57 minutes

4. To go from home to work, Kristen takes
   a train for 1 hour 15 minutes and then a
   subway for 12 minutes. She said her total
   daily commute is 1 hour 27 minutes. Is
   she correct? Explain.

   No; She must also get back home,
   so her daily commute is probably
   about 2 hours 54 minutes.

Copyright © Houghton Mifflin Company. All rights reserved.

Use with text pages 166–167.

Double Bar Graphs

Use the double bar graph to solve Problems 1–5.

1. For which sport is there the greatest difference between the number of girls and boys who participate?

   _____volleyball_____

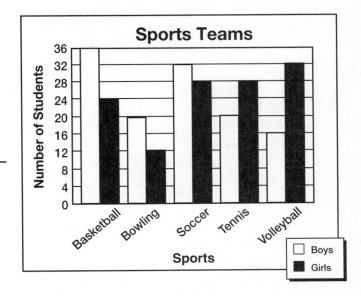

2. How many more boys than girls play basketball?

   _____12_____

3. Suppose that 8 more boys join the tennis team. How would that change the graph?

   Possible answer: The bar for the number of boys would go from 20 to 28 and would be equal to the number of girls on the tennis team.

4. According to the graph, do more boys or girls participate in sports? How many more?

   No; There are 124 boys and 124 girls.

5. What would happen to the double bar graph if the interval for the number of students were changed from 4 to 8? Explain your thinking.

   Possible answer: The differences between the boys' and girls' participation would not look as great.

Copyright © Houghton Mifflin Company. All rights reserved.

Use with text pages 172–175.

Name _____ Date _____

Histograms

Use the histogram to solve Problems 1–5.

1. In which age group have the most presidents been inaugurated?

   _____50–54_____

2. What would happen to the histogram if the interval for the number of presidents were 1 instead of 2?

   Possible answer:
   The size of the bars between the age groups would double.

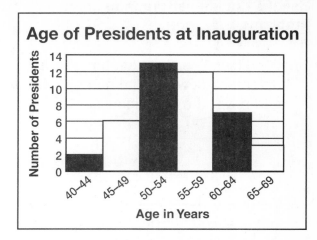

Show Your Work

3. How many more are in the 55–59 age group than in the 40–44 age group?

   _____10 presidents_____

4. Grover Cleveland was 48 years old when he was inaugurated as president in 1885. He served from 1885 to 1889. He was inaugurated again in 1893 and served as president from 1893 to 1897. Could he have been counted in the same age group both times? Explain.

   No. First Term:
   45–49 age group;
   Second term:
   55-59 age group.

5. Suppose Bob Dole, who was 73 years old when he lost the 1996 presidential election to Bill Clinton, had won. Explain how this information would change the histogram.

   Possible answer: An interval from 70–74 would be added.

Copyright © Houghton Mifflin Company. All rights reserved.

Use with text pages 176–177.

Name _____ Date _____

Line and Double Line Graphs

The graph shows the amount the classes needed to raise over the past five years for a school trip. Use the line graph to answer Problems 1–3.

1. How much did the cost of the trip increase from 2000 to 2001?

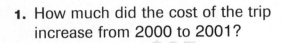
$25

2. Between which two years was there the greatest increase in the cost of the trip?

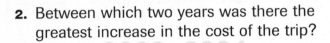
2003–2004

3. Describe the pattern of the cost increase of the trip over the four-year period. What do you predict the trip will cost in 2005? in 2006?

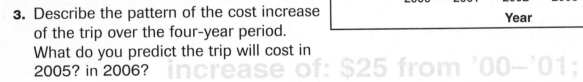
increase of: $25 from '00–'01; $50 '01–'02; $100 '02–'03; $200 '03–'04; $950; $1,750

Cost of Class Trip

This graph shows the amount of money one class raised from September through January. Use the graph to solve Problems 4–5.

4. Which two months had the same amount of sales in both gift cards and wrapping paper?

September and January

5. How much money has the class raised from the sale of gift cards? wrapping paper? both?

$375, $575, $950

Gift Cards and Wrapping Paper Sales

— Gift Cards
- - Wrapping Paper

Copyright © Houghton Mifflin Company. All rights reserved.

Use with text pages 178–180.

Choose an Appropriate Graph

Choose an appropriate graph for the data described in Problems 1–4. Choose from the following: bar graph, histogram, circle graph, line graph, or pictograph.

Show Your Work

1. Box office receipts by age groups.

   histogram

2. The amount of weight George's puppy gained the first six weeks he owned it.

   line graph

3. The parts of Sang's allowance that she spends on entertainment, school supplies, clothes, gifts, and other.

   circle graph

4. Choose and make an appropriate graph for the data given. Explain why you chose to display the data on that type of graph.

   Check graphs; a bar graph or pictograph

Ruling Monarchs of England by Name	
Name	**Number of Kings/Queens**
William	4
Stephen	1
Henry	8
Richard	3
John	1
Edward	8
Mary	2

Copyright © Houghton Mifflin Company. All rights reserved.

Misleading Graphs

Graphs A and B show the same information.
Use them to solve Problems 1–4.

A

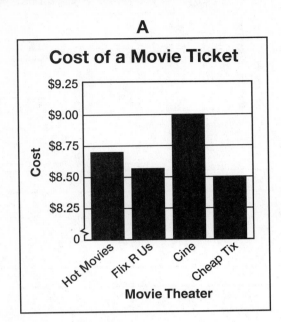

B

Show Your Work

1. Which graph makes the differences in
   price seem greater? Why?

   _____

   Graph A; *Possible answer:*
   It uses small intervals.

2. If you were the owner of Cine, which
   graph would you prefer? Explain.

   _____

   Graph B; *Possible answer:*
   It seems to show less of a
   price difference.

3. How could the owner of Cheap Tix make
   a bar graph to make her movie tickets
   appear even less expensive?

   _____

   Possible answer:
   Use an even smaller
   interval.

4. Which graph do you think displays the
   data in a misleading way? Explain your
   thinking?

   _____

   Possible answer:
   On Graph A Cine looks
   as if it is more expensive
   than Cheap Tix, when it
   is 50 cents more.

Copyright © Houghton Mifflin Company. All rights reserved.

Use with text pages 184–185.

Problem-Solving Decision: Relevant Information

1. Conservation students found the following double bar graph showing the world's top energy producers and users. They needed to compare the greatest energy producing country with the least energy producing country and discover the differences. They did the same comparison with energy users, comparing the greatest with the least.

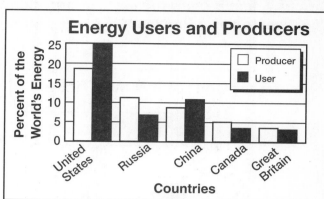

Energy Users and Producers

Producer
User

Percent of the World's Energy

United States   Russia   China   Canada   Great Britain

Countries

UNDERSTAND

What did the students need to find?

The difference between the greatest and least energy producers and users.

PLAN

How could they use relevant information to solve the problem?

_____

Subtract to find both the production and usage differences.

SOLVE

What are the solutions?

_____

19 − 3 = 16 percent
25 − 3 = 22 percent

LOOK BACK

Look back at the information requested. Are your answers reasonable?

_____

Answers will vary.

Use the graph to solve Problem 2.

2. Explain how this graph would help if you are planning a special class lunch and will serve only one type of food.

Possible answer: Pizza is the best choice.

Student's Favorite Lunch

Girls
Boys

Number of Students

Pizza   Hamburger   Taco   Macaroni

Lunch

Copyright © Houghton Mifflin Company. All rights reserved.

Use with text pages 186–187.

Collect and Organize Data

The table shows the results of a survey of
a fifth-grade class. Use the table to solve
Problems 1–5.

Pet	Number of Students With Pet
Dog	卌 |||
Cat	卌 卌
Rabbit	||
Hamster	||||
Guinea pig	|||

Show Your Work

1. Which pet do the most students have?

   cat

2. How many more students have dogs
   than hamsters?

   4 more students

3. What is the frequency for each pet?

   dog: 8, cat: 10, rabbit: 2,
   hamster: 4, guinea pig: 3

4. Suppose there are 22 students in
   Ms. Franklin's class. What does that
   tell you about the table?

   Possible answer: Some of the
   students have more than one type of pet.

5. Can you tell the number of pets that
   each student in the class has? Explain.

   No; *Possible explanation:* The table does
   not show the number of pets per student.
   A student could have 0 pets or a student
   could have 5 pets.

Copyright © Houghton Mifflin Company. All rights reserved.

Use with text pages 192–193.

Name _____ Date _____

Mean, Median, Mode, and Range

Use the following data to solve Problems 1–5.

Number of wins for the Newland High School Hawks each year for the last 10 years: 41, 50, 57, 60, 45, 41, 33, 41, 43, 44.

Show Your Work

1. Make a line plot for the data.

Number of Wins for the Newland Hawks Each Year for the Last 10 Years

33 34 35 36 37 38 39 40 41 42 43 44 45 46 47 48 49 50 51 52 53 54 55 56 57 58 59 60

Check line plots.

2. Are there any clusters or gaps? If so, what are they?

Yes; There is a cluster from 43–45. There are gaps from 34–40, 42, 46–49, 51–56, and 58–59

3. Find the range, median, mode, and mean of the data.

range: 27, median: 43.5, mode: 41, mean: 45.5

4. Eleven years ago, the Hawks won 21 games. What is the median number of wins if that season is included?

43

5. The year the Hawks won 33 games was only a 50-game year. Suppose the Hawks had won 54 games that season. How would the range, median, mode, and mean change?

range: 19, median: 44.5, mode: no change, mean: 47.6

Copyright © Houghton Mifflin Company. All rights reserved.

Use with text pages 194–196.

Make and Use a Stem-and-Leaf Plot

Use the following information for Problems 1–5.

Number of pages Mr. Roberts' students read over the weekend: 82, 43, 39, 41, 29, 45, 91, 33, 59, 43, 37, 47, 72, 60, 62, 38, 42, 56, 42, 89

Show Your Work

1. Make a stem-and-leaf plot of the data.

   Check stem-and-leaf plots.

Number of Pages Mr. Roberts' Students Read Over the Weekend	
Stem	Leaf
2	9
3	3 7 8 9
4	1 2 2 3 3 5 7
5	6 9
6	0 2
7	2
8	2 9
9	1

7|2 means 72.

2. What does 3|9 mean in the stem-and-leaf plot?

   39 pages read over the weekend

3. What was the greatest number of pages read?

   91 pages

4. Find the range, median, and mode of the data.

   range: 62, median: 44, mode: 42 and 43

5. Suppose that an additional student had not read anything over the weekend. How would the stem-and-leaf plot change?

   Possible answer: There would be a stem with 0 and a corresponding leaf with 0, and there would be a stem with a 1 and an empty leaf.

Copyright © Houghton Mifflin Company. All rights reserved.

Use with text pages 198–199.

Problem-Solving Strategy:
Make a Table

Problem These are the years the states other than the 13 colonies entered the Union: 1819, 1959, 1912, 1836, 1850, 1876, 1845, 1959, 1890, 1818, 1816, 1846, 1861, 1792, 1812, 1820, 1837, 1858, 1817, 1821, 1889, 1867, 1864, 1912, 1889, 1803, 1907, 1859, 1889, 1796, 1845, 1896, 1791, 1889, 1863, 1848, 1890

Did most of these states enter the Union between 1791 and 1820, 1821 and 1850, 1851 and 1880, 1881 and 1910, 1911 and 1940, or 1941 and 1970?

UNDERSTAND

What is the question?

See question above.

What information does the problem give you?

the years each state entered the Union

PLAN

How can a table help solve the problem?

Answers will vary.

SOLVE

Which range of years should you use in the table?

See table.

Fill in the ranges of years on the table.

Use tally marks to record the number of states entering the Union for each interval.

Count the tally marks and write the frequencies.

What is the solution?

between 1791 and 1820

Years	Number of States that Entered the Union	Frequency
1791–1820	ＷＨ ＷＨ	10
1821–1850	ＷＨ ＩＩＩ	8
1851–1880	ＷＨ ＩＩ	7
1881–1910	ＷＨ ＩＩＩ	8
1911–1940	ＩＩ	2
1941–1970	ＩＩ	2

LOOK BACK

How can you check your answer?

Answers will vary.

Copyright © Houghton Mifflin Company. All rights reserved.

Use with text pages 200–202.

Draw Conclusions and Make Predictions

Use the data to solve Problems 1–5.

Dave took 12 typing tests to see how many words he could type per minute. He scored 42, 44, 41, 39, 55, 40, 46, 40, 46, 48, 41, and 46.

Show Your Work

1. Find Dave's mean, median, and mode scores.

   _____ 44, 43, 46 _____

2. What do you think Dave will score on his next typing test? Why?

   Possible answer: 44; this is his mean score.

3. If Dave wants to convince his classmates that he is an excellent typist, should he use the mean, median, or mode? Explain.

   Dave should use the mode; Possible explanation: It is the greatest score.

4. Anjalie's mean score on 4 typing tests is 80. What does she need to score on each of the next 4 tests to raise her mean score to 90?

   She needs to score 100 on each of the next 4 tests.

5. Suppose Dave scores 50 and 52 on his next two tests. Find the new mean, median, and mode. Then predict what Dave's next typing test score will be. Explain your prediction.

   mean: 45, median; 45, mode: 46; 45 Possible explanation: The new mean and median are both 45, so his next score will probably be 45.

Copyright © Houghton Mifflin Company. All rights reserved.

Use with text pages 204–206.

Prime and Composite Numbers

Show Your Work

1. I am a number between 60 and 100. My ones digit is two less than my tens digit. I am a prime number. What number am I?

   _____97_____

2. The sum of my ones digit and tens digit is 10. My tens digit is greater than my ones digit. I am a prime number. What number am I?

   _____73_____

3. The sum of my ones digit and tens digit is also 10. However, my ones digit is greater than my tens digit. I am a prime number less than 30. What number am I?

   _____19_____

4. Not including myself and 1, my factors are 2, 3, 4, 6, 8, 12, 16, 24, 32, and 48. What number am I?

   _____96_____

5. Husam has 30 baseball cards. He wants to arrange them in equal rows. In how many ways can he arrange them?

   _____8_____

6. Other than 2 and 3, can two consecutive whole numbers be prime numbers? Explain why or why not.

   No; *Possible answer:* one of the two numbers will always have 2 for a factor and will not be prime.

Copyright © Houghton Mifflin Company. All rights reserved.

Use with text pages 224–225.

Prime Factorization

Show Your Work

1. Which number between 20 and 29 has 2 and 3 in its prime factorization?

_____24_____

2. Which number between 29 and 39 has three different prime factors? What is the prime factorization of this number?

30; 2 × 3 × 5

3. Which numbers between 40 and 49 have 2 and 3 in their prime factorization? Use exponents to write the prime factorization of each number.

48; $2^4 \times 3^1$ and 42; $2^1 \times 3^1 \times 7^1$

4. Tony said the prime factorization of 72 is $2^3 \times 3^3$. Explain what Tony's mistake was. Then find the correct answer.

Tony found the
prime factorization
of 216; $2^3 \times 3^2$.

5. Can a number greater than 100 have only 1 number in its prime factorization? Explain why or why not.

Yes; *Possible answer:* Any prime number that is
raised to an exponent will have only 1 number
in its prime factorization. For example, the
prime factorization of 125 is 5^3.

Copyright © Houghton Mifflin Company. All rights reserved.

Use with text pages 226–227.

Greatest Common Factor

1. The GCF of an odd number and an even number is 33. The greater number is 99. Find the other number.

_____ 66 _____

2. Ms. Booth is sewing dresses. She has 16 red buttons and 24 blue buttons. Each dress will have the same number of blue and red buttons. Using all buttons, what is the greatest number of dresses Ms. Booth can sew?

_____ 8 dresses _____

3. What is the greatest common factor that two numbers between 40 and 50 have?

_____ 7 (42 and 49) _____

4. In the lunchroom, 36 fifth-graders and 27 fourth-graders are sitting in equal groups. All the students in each group are in the same grade. What is the greatest number of students who could be in each group?

_____ 9 _____

5. Sheila says the GCF of 36 and 72 is 18. Explain Sheila's mistake. Then tell the correct answer.

_____

18 is a common factor of 36 and 72, but not the greatest common factor; the GCF is 36.

Copyright © Houghton Mifflin Company. All rights reserved.

Use with text pages 228–230.

Least Common Multiple

Show Your Work

1. Nick and Inez are running around a
1-mile loop in the park. Nick runs an
8-minute mile and Inez runs a
10-minute mile. If they start together,
how long will it take Nick to pass Inez
a second time?

   _____ 40 minutes _____

2. Willis has a guitar lesson every 3 days
and a piano lesson every 5 days. How
often does he have a guitar and a piano
lesson on the same day?

   _____ every 15 days _____

3. Anna said the LCM of 8 and 12 is 4.
Explain what Anna's mistake was. Then
tell the correct answer.

   _____ Anna found the greatest
   common factor, not the
   LCM; the LCM of 8 and
   12 is 24. _____

4. When can the LCM of two numbers be
one of those numbers? Give an example.

   _____ The LCM can be one of the two
   numbers when the greater number is
   a multiple of the lesser number. For
   example, the LCM of 4 and 8 is 8. _____

5. Can the LCM and the GCF of two numbers be the same number? Explain why
or why not.

   _____ No; Explanations will vary. _____

Copyright © Houghton Mifflin Company. All rights reserved.

Use with text pages 232–234.

Name _____ Date _____

Fractions and Mixed Numbers

Show Your Work

1. The Terriers softball team has 15 players. Three players are sick and cannot play in the next game. What fraction of the team can play in the next game?

$$\frac{12}{15}$$

2. Carol pitches for the Terriers. In the last game, she got 14 outs before an opponent reached base. There are 3 outs in one inning. How many innings did Carol pitch before an opponent reached base? Write your answer as a mixed number.

$$4\frac{2}{3}$$

3. The Terriers won 8 games and lost 5 this season. What fraction of their games has the team won?

$$\frac{8}{13}$$

4. Bryon said that $6\overline{)19}$ is the same as $\frac{19}{6}$. Is he correct? Explain why or why not.

Yes; Possible explanation: $6\overline{)19}$ is the same as 19 divided by 6, and $\frac{19}{6}$ is also the same as 19 divided by 6.

5. Do $\frac{2}{3}$ and $\frac{3}{2}$ name the same fraction? Explain why or why not.

No; Possible answer: $\frac{2}{3}$ is less than 1 and $\frac{3}{2}$ is greater than 1.

Copyright © Houghton Mifflin Company. All rights reserved.

Use with text pages 236–238.

Name _____   Date _____

Equivalent Fractions and Simplest Form

Problem Solving 9.6

Show Your Work

1. Mr. Jackson always works every week-day in June. In 2005, the month of June had 22 weekdays. What fraction of the days in June of 2005 did Mr. Jackson work? Write your answer in simplest form.

_____ $\frac{11}{15}$

2. A nurse works 2 out of every 3 days. Fill in the boxes to continue the pattern of days she must work. $\frac{2}{3}, \frac{4}{6}, \frac{\square}{9}, \frac{8}{\square}, \frac{\square}{\square}$

_____ 6; 12; $\frac{10}{15}$ _____

3. Mary Lou said that $\frac{16}{20}$ in simplest form is $\frac{8}{10}$. Explain what Mary Lou's mistake was. Then tell the correct answer.

Mary Lou found an equivalent fraction, but not one in simplest form; $\frac{4}{5}$.

4. Trish walks 15 blocks to school. If she walks $\frac{2}{10}$ of the way by herself, how many blocks does she walk by herself? How many blocks does she walk with others?

_____ 3; 12 _____

5. Can a fraction with a numerator of 1 be simplified? Explain why or why not.

No; *Possible explanation:* The GCF of 1 and any other number is 1, which is the definition of simplest form.

Copyright © Houghton Mifflin Company. All rights reserved.

Use with text pages 240–241.

Problem-Solving Strategy:
Use Logical Reasoning

Problem The GCF of two numbers is 5. The LCM of the same two numbers is 75. The numbers differ by 10. What are the numbers?

UNDERSTAND

What is the question?

What are the numbers?

What facts does the problem give you?

The GCF is 5, the LCM is 75, the numbers differ by 10.

PLAN

How can you use logical reasoning to solve this problem?

Possible answer: Draw a Venn diagram to represent all the factors. Factor 75 and find the factors that match the facts of the problem.

SOLVE

Draw a Venn diagram and put the GCF in the Venn diagram.

Check diagrams: Venn diagram with 5 in overlap space

What is the prime factorization of 75?

_3 × 5 × 5_

Which pair of factors have a difference of 10 and a GCF of 5?

15 and 25

What is the solution?

15 and 25

LOOK BACK

How can you check your answer?

The GCF of 15 and 25 is 5, the LCM is 75, and 25 − 15 = 10, so the numbers match all the facts given in the problem.

Copyright © Houghton Mifflin Company. All rights reserved.

Use with text pages 242–245.

Relate Fractions, Mixed Numbers, and Decimals

Show Your Work

1. Trevor started studying at 6:00 P.M. and finished at 9:30 P.M. How many hours did he study? Write your answer as a decimal and as a mixed number in simplest form.

3.5 hours; $3\frac{1}{2}$ hours

2. On his math test, Trevor got 23 out of 25 questions correct. Write the correct fraction as a decimal.

0.92

3. Trevor's parents got a mortgage rate of about 6.35. Write the decimal as a mixed number in simplest form.

$6\frac{7}{20}$

4. Trevor lives 4.6 miles from school. Write the distance as a mixed number in simplest form.

$4\frac{3}{5}$ miles

5. Trevor says that $\frac{5}{8}$ and 0.6 represent the same number because $\frac{5}{8} = \frac{25}{40}$ and $0.6 = \frac{25}{40}$. Do you agree? Explain your reasoning.

No; Possible explanation: $\frac{5}{8} = \frac{25}{40}$ but $0.6 = \frac{24}{40}$.

Copyright © Houghton Mifflin Company. All rights reserved.

Use with text pages 246–247.

Compare and Order Fractions and Decimals

Show Your Work

1. The students in Ms. Gumb's class are selling candy bars for a class trip. Each student received the same number to sell. Tina has sold $\frac{2}{3}$ of hers and Carrie has sold 0.7 of hers. Who has sold more candy bars?

   _____Carrie_____

2. Mollie wants to sell the most candy bars. She has sold $\frac{4}{5}$ of hers. Has she sold more than Carrie? Explain your answer.

   Yes; $\frac{4}{5}$ = 0.8 and 0.8 > 0.7

3. Marco is 5.5 feet tall, Steve is $5\frac{5}{8}$ feet tall, and Susan is $5\frac{2}{5}$ feet tall. Order the students from shortest to tallest.

   Susan, Marco, Steve

4. Jim ate $\frac{3}{8}$ of a pie and Jung ate 0.4 of the same pie. Who ate more pie?

   _____Jung_____

5. Without using equivalent fractions, explain how you can tell that $\frac{12}{25} < \frac{7}{13}$.

   Possible answer: You can compare both fractions to $\frac{1}{2}$: $\frac{12}{25}$ is less than $\frac{1}{2}$ and $\frac{7}{13}$ is greater than $\frac{1}{2}$.

Copyright © Houghton Mifflin Company. All rights reserved.

Use with text pages 248–250.

Estimate With Fractions

Show Your Work

1. Lauren wants to know if her sofa and 2 end tables will fit along a wall that is 10 feet long. Her sofa is $5\frac{1}{2}$ feet long, and each end table is $1\frac{3}{4}$ feet long. Will all the furniture fit? Explain your answer.

   Yes; *Possible answer:* $5\frac{1}{2} + 1\frac{3}{4} + 1\frac{3}{4}$ is about $9\frac{1}{2}$, which is less than 10.

2. Keisha's dog Honey grew from $25\frac{1}{2}$ pounds to $30\frac{1}{4}$ pounds last month. About how many pounds did Honey gain?

   Possible answer: about 5 pounds

3. Keisha and Honey jog together. In one week, they ran $1\frac{3}{4}$ miles, $1\frac{2}{5}$ miles, $\frac{1}{2}$ mile, 1 mile, and $1\frac{1}{4}$ miles. About how many miles did they run in all?

   Possible answer: about 6 miles

4. Honey was $16\frac{1}{4}$ inches tall when Keisha adopted her. Now Honey is $24\frac{3}{8}$ inches tall. About how many inches has Honey grown?

   Possible answer: about 8 inches

5. When estimating $2\frac{1}{5} + 1\frac{7}{8}$, would it make sense to round each mixed number to the nearest ten? Explain why or why not.

   No; *Possible answer:* Both numbers round to 0 when rounded to the nearest ten.

Copyright © Houghton Mifflin Company. All rights reserved.

Use with text pages 256–257.

Name _____ Date _____

Add With Like Denominators

Show Your Work

1. On a greatest hits CD, $\frac{3}{16}$ of the songs are from the 1950s, and $\frac{10}{16}$ of the songs are from the 1960s. What fraction of the songs are from the 1950s and 1960s combined?

_____ $\frac{13}{16}$ _____

2. On a different CD, $\frac{3}{8}$ of the songs are rock songs, and $\frac{2}{8}$ of the songs are ballads. What fraction of the CD's songs are rock songs and ballads combined?

_____ $\frac{5}{8}$ _____

3. Brenda spent $\frac{3}{4}$ of an hour alphabetizing her CDs and another $3\frac{3}{4}$ hours organizing the names of the CDs in a database. How many hours did Brenda spend on her CDs? Write your answer in simplest form.

_____ $4\frac{1}{2}$ hours _____

4. Is $\frac{3}{4} + \frac{3}{4}$ the same as $\frac{6}{8} + \frac{6}{8}$? Explain your answer. Yes; Possible answer: $\frac{3}{4}$ and $\frac{6}{8}$ are equivalent, so the answer will be the same: $\frac{3}{4} + \frac{3}{4} = \frac{6}{4} = 1\frac{1}{2}$ and $\frac{6}{8} + \frac{6}{8} = \frac{12}{8} = 1\frac{1}{2}$.

5. In a rock band, $\frac{5}{10}$ of the band members play guitar and $\frac{2}{10}$ play keyboards. Joe wrote that $\frac{7}{20}$ of the band members play guitar or keyboards. Explain what Joe's mistake was. What fraction of the band members play guitar or keyboards? Joe added the denominators; $\frac{7}{10}$

Copyright © Houghton Mifflin Company. All rights reserved.

Use with text pages 258–259.

Add Fractions With Unlike Denominators

Show Your Work

1. A recipe for marinade calls for $\frac{1}{2}$ teaspoon of chili powder and $\frac{1}{4}$ teaspoon of garlic powder. How many teaspoons of chili powder and garlic powder combined are needed?

   $\frac{3}{4}$ teaspoon

2. An apricot and banana bread recipe calls for $\frac{1}{4}$ cup of chopped apricots and $\frac{3}{8}$ cup of mashed bananas. How many cups of fruit are in this recipe?

   $\frac{5}{8}$ cup

3. The apricot and banana bread takes $\frac{3}{4}$ of an hour to bake. The marinade takes about $\frac{1}{12}$ of an hour to prepare. How long will it take to bake the apricot and banana bread and then prepare the marinade? Write your answer in simplest form.

   $\frac{5}{6}$ hour

4. At the deli, Jon got $\frac{3}{4}$ pound of ham and $\frac{7}{16}$ pound of turkey. How many pounds of meat did Jon get?

   $1\frac{3}{16}$ pounds

5. Jon walked $\frac{1}{5}$ of a mile to the deli. On the way home, he took a different route and walked $\frac{1}{4}$ of a mile. How far did he walk in all?

   $\frac{9}{20}$ mile

Copyright © Houghton Mifflin Company. All rights reserved.

Use with text pages 260–261.

Add Mixed Numbers With Unlike Denominators

Show Your Work

1. Denise baked $2\frac{1}{2}$ trays of sugar cookies and $1\frac{3}{4}$ trays of peanut butter cookies. How many trays of cookies did she bake in all?

   _____$4\frac{1}{4}$ trays_____

2. Denise also baked $2\frac{1}{4}$ trays of chocolate chip cookies and $1\frac{1}{2}$ trays of oatmeal raisin cookies. Including the trays in Problem 1, how many trays did she bake altogether?

   _____8 trays_____

3. Suppose that Denise had doubled the number of trays of chocolate chip and oatmeal raisin cookies she baked. How many trays of cookies would she have baked?

   _____$4\frac{1}{2}$ trays of chocolate chip cookies, and 3 trays of oatmeal raisin cookies_____

4. Before baking the cookies, Denise spent $2\frac{1}{2}$ hours doing laundry, $1\frac{5}{12}$ hours cleaning the house, and $1\frac{1}{4}$ hours grocery shopping. How many hours did Denise spend on these activities in all? Write your answer in simplest form.

   _____$5\frac{1}{6}$ hours_____

Copyright © Houghton Mifflin Company. All rights reserved.

Use with text pages 262–264.

Subtract With Like Denominators

Show Your Work

1. In a recent baseball game, the starting
pitcher played for $6\frac{2}{3}$ innings. If the
game lasted 9 innings, how many
innings did the relief pitchers pitch?

_____ $2\frac{1}{3}$ innings

2. The first relief pitcher played for
$1\frac{1}{3}$ innings. How much longer did the
starting pitcher play than the first relief
pitcher?

_____ $5\frac{1}{3}$ innings _____

3. The second relief pitcher played for
$\frac{2}{3}$ inning. How much longer did the
first relief pitcher play than the second
relief pitcher?

_____ $\frac{2}{3}$ inning _____

4. Find the number of innings that the starting pitcher and two relief pitchers played
in all. If the closing pitcher played for the
remainder of the 9-inning game, how
many innings did the closing pitcher play?

_____ $\frac{1}{3}$ inning

5. Suppose that the starting pitcher played
for $7\frac{1}{3}$ innings and the game lasted
12 innings. How many innings would
the relief pitchers have to pitch? Explain
the steps you took to find your answer.

$4\frac{2}{3}$ innings; *Possible answer:*
I subtracted $7\frac{1}{3}$ from 12, the number
of innings in the whole game.

Copyright © Houghton Mifflin Company. All rights reserved.

Use with text pages 266–267.

Name _____   Date _____

Subtract With Unlike Denominators

Show Your Work

1. In Ms. Harmon's class, $\frac{1}{2}$ of the boys like watching cartoons and $\frac{1}{3}$ of the girls like watching cartoons. How much greater is the fractional part of the boys than the fractional part of the girls who like watching cartoons?

   $\frac{1}{6}$

2. In a survey of bedtimes, $\frac{3}{5}$ of the students said their bedtime is between 9 P.M. and 9:59 P.M. and $\frac{1}{4}$ said their bedtime is between 10 P.M. and 10:59 P.M. How much greater is the fractional part of the students who go to sleep at the earlier time?

   $\frac{7}{20}$

3. Monica computed $\frac{5}{16} - \frac{1}{4}$ and found $\frac{4}{12}$, or $\frac{1}{3}$. Explain what Monica's mistake was. Then tell the correct answer.

   Possible answer: Monica subtracted the denominators as well as the numerators; $\frac{1}{16}$.

3. Ms. Harmon's science lesson lasts $\frac{3}{4}$ of an hour. So far $\frac{5}{12}$ of an hour has elapsed. What fraction of an hour remains of Ms. Harmon's science lesson? Write your answer in simplest form. Then explain your answer.

   $\frac{1}{3}$ hour; Possible answer: The LCD of $\frac{3}{4}$ and $\frac{5}{12}$ is 12, so rewrite $\frac{3}{4} - \frac{5}{12}$ as $\frac{9}{12} - \frac{5}{12}$. $\frac{9}{12} - \frac{5}{12} = \frac{4}{12}$ and $\frac{4}{12}$ in simplest form is $\frac{1}{3}$.

Copyright © Houghton Mifflin Company. All rights reserved.

Use with text pages 268–269.

Problem-Solving Strategy:
Draw a Diagram

Problem In the election for class president, Joanie received $\frac{4}{5}$ of the votes. That was four times as many votes as Artie. How many more votes did Joanie get?

UNDERSTAND

1. What is the question?
_____

How much greater was the fraction of votes Joanie received?

2. What facts does the problem tell you?
_____

Joanie received $\frac{4}{5}$ of the votes and she received 4 times as many votes as Artie.

PLAN

3. How could drawing a diagram help you solve this problem?
_____

a diagram can compare the fraction of votes Joanie received with the fraction of votes Artie received.

SOLVE

4. This strip represents all the votes:

Draw a strip to represent Joanie's votes.

5. Draw a strip to represent Artie's votes. | |

6. What fraction of the votes did Artie receive?

$\frac{1}{5}$ of the votes

7. What is the solution?
_____
$\frac{3}{5}$

LOOK BACK

8. How do you know your answer is reasonable?

$\frac{1}{5} \times 4 = \frac{4}{5}$, so Artie received $\frac{1}{5}$ of the votes. And $\frac{4}{5} - \frac{1}{5} = \frac{3}{5}$.

Copyright © Houghton Mifflin Company. All rights reserved.

Use with text pages 270–272.

Name _____   Date _____

Subtract Mixed Numbers With Unlike Denominators

Show Your Work

1. Bud bought a new door that is $31\frac{1}{4}$ inches wide. A door wider than $29\frac{1}{2}$ inches wide will not fit in his doorframe. How many inches of the new door will Bud have to remove?

   _____ $1\frac{3}{4}$ inches _____

2. The new door he bought is $75\frac{1}{8}$ inches tall. How many inches taller is the door than it is wide?

   _____ $43\frac{7}{8}$ inches _____

3. Bart computed $8\frac{5}{7} - 4\frac{6}{7}$ and found $4\frac{6}{7}$. Explain what Bart's mistake was. Then tell the correct answer.

   _____ Bart did not regroup $8\frac{5}{7}$ to $7\frac{12}{7}$; $3\frac{6}{7}$ _____

4. Bud worked $17\frac{3}{4}$ hours doing odd jobs this week. He worked $36\frac{1}{2}$ hours at his regular job. How many more hours did he work at his regular job than doing odd jobs? Explain how you found your answer.

   _____

   $18\frac{3}{4}$ hours; Possible answer: Set up subtraction problem: $36\frac{1}{2} - 17\frac{3}{4}$. Find LCD and regroup to $35\frac{6}{4} - 17\frac{3}{4}$. Subtract fractions: $\frac{6}{4} - \frac{3}{4} = \frac{3}{4}$. Subtract whole numbers: $35 - 17 = 18$. Add whole number and fraction: $18 + \frac{3}{4} = 18\frac{3}{4}$.

Copyright © Houghton Mifflin Company. All rights reserved.

Use with text pages 274–276.

Explore Addition and Subtraction With Decimals

Show Your Work

1. During the 1999–2000 hockey season, a Philadelphia Flyers goalie allowed 1.91 goals per game. His teammate allowed 2.20 goals per game. How many fewer goals per game did the goalie allow than his teammate?

0.29 goals per game

2. During the 2000 soccer season, the goalkeeper for the Kansas City Wizards gave up just 0.92 goal per game. The goalkeeper for the Los Angeles Galaxy gave up 1.00 goal per game. How many goals per game better was the Wizards goalkeeper?

0.08 goal per game

3. In 2000 the leading scorer on the Chicago Fire averaged 1.75 points per game. The best scorer in the league averaged 0.26 more points per game. How many points per game did the best scorer average?

2.01 points per game

4. Jenny wants to buy tickets to the Sacramento Kings versus Portland Trailblazers game. Each ticket costs $22.50. Jenny has $100. What is the greatest number of tickets that Jenny can buy? Will she have money left over? Explain your answers.

Jenny can buy up to 4 tickets. She will have $10.00 left. *Possible answer:* I subtracted $22.50 from $100.00 four times and was left with $10.00.

Copyright © Houghton Mifflin Company. All rights reserved.

Use with text pages 282–283.

Add Decimals

Show Your Work

1. Ross makes $12.50 per hour at his job
   at the bakery. If he gets a raise of
   $1.45 per hour, how much will Ross
   make per hour?

   _____$13.95_____

2. Ross worked 37.25 hours last week and
   32.25 hours this week. How many hours
   has Ross worked altogether?

   _____69.5 hours_____

3. Today Ross drove 3.8 miles to work, 2.6
   miles to a friend's house, and 3.8 miles
   back home. How many miles did Ross
   drive in all?

   _____10.2 miles_____

4. Can the sum of two decimals to the
   thousandths place ever equal a whole
   number? Explain your answer.

   Yes; Possible answer: two decimals to the
   thousandths place can equal a whole number;
   for example, $0.725 + 0.275 = 1$

5. Britney added 1.625 and 0.43 and got
   1.668. Explain what Britney's mistake
   was. Then tell the correct answer.

   Possible answer: Britney did not line up the
   decimal points correctly; 2.055

Copyright © Houghton Mifflin Company. All rights reserved.

Use with text pages 284–285.

Name _____ Date _____

Subtract Decimals

Show Your Work

1. In 2002 a player on the Portland Fire led the WNBA in shooting at 0.629. That was 0.068 better than the second place finisher of the Minnesota Lynx. What did the Lynx player shoot?

   0.561

2. In the 2002 season, the Los Angeles Sparks were the WNBA's top team. The team won 0.75 of its games. The league's worst team, the Detroit Shock, won 0.281 of its games. What decimal describes how many more games the Sparks won than the Shock?

   0.469

3. In 2002 a player on the Washington Mystics was the WNBA's leading scorer. She scored an average of 19.85 points per game. That average was 2.25 points per game better than her career average. What is this player's career average?

   17.6 points per game

4. The average points-per-player in the 2002 WNBA playoff games was about 12.897. The lowest number of points-per-player was 8.0 and the highest number was 24.3. How much greater is the average than the lowest points-per-player? How much greater is the highest points-per-player than the average? Explain the method you used to solve each problem.

   4.897; 11.403. Possible answer: Subtracted the lowest score (8.0) from the average (12.897); Subtracted the average (12.897) from the highest score (24.3).

Copyright © Houghton Mifflin Company. All rights reserved.

Use with text pages 286–288.

Estimate Decimal Sums and Differences

1–2: *Estimates may vary.*

Use the data from the chart to solve Problems 1–3.

Average Annual Precipitation of 5 U.S. Cities	
City	Average Annual Precipitation (in inches)
Mobile, Alabama	63.96
Chicago, Illinois	35.82
Miami, Florida	55.91
Memphis, Tennessee	52.10
Raleigh, North Carolina	41.43

Show Your Work

1. Estimate how many more inches of precipitation Mobile averages than Chicago to the nearest inch.

   28 inches

2. Estimate how many more inches of precipitation Mobile averages than Chicago to the nearest tenth of an inch.

   28.2 inches

3. If you were estimating the total precipitation for all the cities in the chart, would it make sense to round each number to the nearest ten inches? Explain why or why not. Yes. *Possible answer:* All of the cities have precipitation totals greater than 10 and less than 100, so rounding to the nearest 10 will give usable information.

4. How is estimating decimals like estimating whole numbers? How is it different?
   Possible answer: Estimating decimals and whole numbers, use the same rounding rules. Estimating whole numbers, round to the nearest 10, 100, etc.; When estimating decimals, round to a place less than 1.

Copyright © Houghton Mifflin Company. All rights reserved.

Use with text pages 290–291.

Problem-Solving Decision:
Choose a Method

1. On a business trip, Dom spent $143.32 on a hotel, $82.48 on meals, $295.18 on transportation, and $11.23 on phone calls. How much did Dom spend on his trip?

UNDERSTAND

What is the question?

How much money did Dom spend on his trip?

What facts does the problem tell you?

Dom spent $143.32 on a hotel, $82.48 on meals, $295.18 on transportation, and $11.23 on phone calls.

PLAN

Which computation method would you use? Explain your choice.

Possible answer: calculator. There are a lot of numbers so I would use a calculator.

SOLVE

What is the solution?

$532.21

LOOK BACK

Is your answer reasonable?

Possible answer: Yes, the answer is reasonable. If I estimate $140 + 80 + 300 + 11 = $531, $532.21 is a reasonable answer.

Choose a method. Then solve.

2. On the same business trip, Brigid spent $410.74. Use the information above to find how much more Dom spent than Brigid.

$121.47

Copyright © Houghton Mifflin Company. All rights reserved.

Use with text pages 292–293.

Model Multiplication

Use models to solve Problems 1–5.

Show Your Work

1. In Ron's CD collection, $\frac{1}{2}$ of the CDs are rock and roll and $\frac{2}{3}$ of those feature male lead singers. What fraction of Ron's CDs have rock and roll male lead singers?

   _____ $\frac{1}{3}$ _____

2. One third of Ron's CDs are country and $\frac{3}{4}$ of those feature female lead singers. What fraction of Ron's CDs have country female lead singers?

   _____ $\frac{1}{4}$ _____

3. Ay-Jiuan used the information from Problem 2 to say that $\frac{1}{4}$ of Ron's total CD collection features country male lead singers. Explain what Ay-Jiuan's mistake was. Then tell what the correct answer is.

   Ay-Jiuan mixed up the country female and male singers; $\frac{1}{12}$.

4. Dawn joined a CD club and got 12 free CDs. If $\frac{5}{6}$ of those CDs were classical, how many classical CDs did Dawn get?

   _____ 10 _____

5. Tim said that the product of a mixed number and a fraction less than one is always greater than the fraction and less than the mixed number. Is he right? Explain why or why not.

   5. Tim is correct. *Possible answer:* The mixed number is greater than 1, so the product is greater than the fraction. The fraction is less than 1, so the product is less than the mixed number. For example, $1\frac{1}{2} \times \frac{1}{4} = \frac{3}{8}$.

Copyright © Houghton Mifflin Company. All rights reserved.

Use with text pages 310–313.

Multiply Fractions

Show Your Work

1. LaToya is having a party. She wants to buy enough juice for each person to have $\frac{1}{2}$ liter. If 24 people are going to be at her party, how many liters of juice does LaToya need to buy?

_____ 12 _____

2. At LaToya's party, $\frac{7}{12}$ of the guests will be girls. Use the information in Problem 1 to decide if there will be more than 13 girls at the party. How do you know?

Yes; $\frac{7}{12} \times 24 = 14$, $14 > 13$

3. Elyssa is baking three different types of cookies for the party. She will make $\frac{5}{8}$ of them chocolate chip, and $\frac{2}{3}$ of those cookies will have nuts. What fraction of the cookies will be chocolate chip with nuts?

_____ $\frac{5}{12}$ _____

4. Kenny is buying 5 pizzas for LaToya's party. If the boys at the party eat $\frac{3}{5}$ of the pizzas, how many pizzas will the boys eat?

_____ 3 _____

5. Jamal said he would bring $\frac{3}{4}$ of the 8 cold sandwiches for the party and Jill said she would bring $\frac{2}{3}$ of the 9 hot sandwiches. Who will bring more sandwiches? Explain your answer.

Possible answer: They will bring the same number of sandwiches: $\frac{3}{4} \times 8 = 6$ and $\frac{2}{3} \times 9 = 6$.

Copyright © Houghton Mifflin Company. All rights reserved.

Name _____ Date _____

Multiply With Mixed Numbers

Show Your Work

1. Phil mows $6\frac{1}{2}$ acres of lawn each day. If he mows $\frac{2}{5}$ of the lawn before lunch, how many acres does he have to mow after lunch?

   _____$3\frac{9}{10}$ acres_____

2. Terrance must decide which job offer to accept. One job pays $25 per hour for $37\frac{1}{2}$ hours each week and the other pays $825 per week regardless of how many hours he works. Which job should Terrance take?

   Possible answer: $25 for $37\frac{1}{2}$ hours pays $937.50, so Terrance should take that one.

3. Debbie is painting a fence that is $8\frac{1}{4}$ times as wide as she is tall. If Debbie is $5\frac{1}{2}$ feet tall, how many feet wide is the fence?

   _____$45\frac{3}{8}$ feet wide_____

4. Scott is a disc jockey at the local radio station. The current number one song is played 12 times each day. If the song is $4\frac{1}{5}$ minutes long, how many minutes a day is the song aired?

   _____$50\frac{2}{5}$ minutes each day_____

5. Can the product of two mixed numbers ever be a whole number? If so, give an example.

   _____Yes; for example, $2\frac{1}{2} \times 4\frac{2}{5} = 11$._____

Copyright © Houghton Mifflin Company. All rights reserved.

Use with text pages 316–318.

Model Division

Use models to solve Problems 1–5.

Show Your Work

1. One period in a hockey game is 20 minutes. Each period makes up $\frac{1}{3}$ of the game. How many minutes long is the game?

   _____ 60 minutes _____

2. Twenty minutes of playing time makes up $\frac{1}{2}$ of a NCAA women's basketball game. How many minutes long is a game?

   _____ 40 minutes _____

3. If you divide $\frac{1}{4}$ of a dollar into parts that are $\frac{1}{20}$ of a dollar, how many parts are there? What are they called?

   _____ 5 parts; nickels _____

4. Manny said that $8 \div \frac{1}{4}$ is equal to $\frac{1}{8} \times 4$. Explain what Manny's mistake was. Then tell the correct answer.

   _____ *Possible answer:* Manny probably meant to say that $8 \div \frac{1}{4}$ is equal to 8×4; 32

5. Can the quotient of two fractions be less than 1? Explain and include an example.

   _____ Yes; *Possible answer:* If the dividend is less than the divisor, the quotient of two fractions will be less than 1, for example, $\frac{1}{4} \div \frac{1}{2} = \frac{1}{2}$.

Copyright © Houghton Mifflin Company. All rights reserved.

Name _____ Date _____

Divide Fractions

Show Your Work

1. Francesca has $12. If she exchanges the $12 for quarters, how many quarters will she receive? Remember that each quarter is $\frac{1}{4}$ of a dollar.

   _____ 48 quarters _____

2. Ms. Hoffman owns $\frac{3}{4}$ acre of property. If she splits her property into two equal sections to give to her daughters, how many acres will each daughter receive?

   _____ $\frac{3}{8}$ acre _____

3. Ms. Hoffman owns $\frac{1}{5}$ the amount of property that her brother owns. Use the information from Problem 2 to find how much property her brother owns.

   _____ $3\frac{3}{4}$ acres _____

4. Which division problem below results in a quotient of 8? What is the other quotient?

   $4 \div \frac{1}{2}$

   $\frac{1}{2} \div 4$

   _____ $4 \div \frac{1}{2}; \frac{1}{8}$ _____

5. Paula said that $\frac{5}{8} \div \frac{1}{2}$ equals $\frac{5}{16}$. Explain what Paula's mistake was. Then tell the correct answer.

   _____ Paula forgot to use the reciprocal of $\frac{1}{2}$ to divide; $1\frac{1}{4}$. _____

Copyright © Houghton Mifflin Company. All rights reserved.

Use with text pages 322–323.

Divide Mixed Numbers

1. Mr. Gittens spent $9\frac{3}{4}$ hours commuting last week. If he commuted $3\frac{1}{4}$ hours each day, how many days did Mr. Gittens commute?

   _____3 days_____

2. Don's round-trip train commute takes $2\frac{1}{2}$ hours each day. If each one-way trip takes the same amount of time, how many hours is each one-way trip?

   _____$1\frac{1}{4}$ hours_____

3. Tracey is in school for $6\frac{2}{3}$ hours each day. Each class lasts $\frac{5}{6}$ of an hour. How many classes does Tracey have each day?

   _____8 classes_____

4. Kathleen measured her pencil to $3\frac{1}{2}$ inches. She then measured her pencil using $\frac{1}{8}$ of an inch as a guide. She said her pencil was $28\frac{1}{8}$s of an inch. Is she correct? Explain.

   Kathleen is correct;
   $3\frac{1}{2} \div \frac{1}{8} = 28$

5. Is the quotient of a mixed number divided by a mixed number greater than or less than 1? Explain.

   5. Possible answer: The quotient of a mixed number can be greater than 1 or less than 1. If the dividend is greater than the divisor, the quotient will be greater than 1. If the dividend is less than the divisor, the quotient will be less than 1.

Copyright © Houghton Mifflin Company. All rights reserved.

Name _____   Date _____

Problem-Solving Decision:
Choose the Operation

1. Suppose that Lauren spent $\frac{1}{2}$ of her homework time working on math. What fractional part of her Monday did she spend doing math homework?

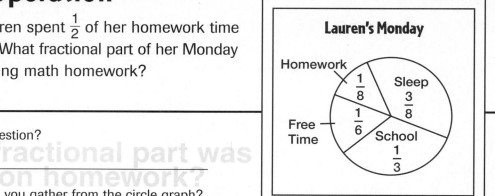

Lauren's Monday

Homework $\frac{1}{8}$ · Sleep $\frac{3}{8}$ · Free Time $\frac{1}{6}$ · School $\frac{1}{3}$

UNDERSTAND

What is the question?

What fractional part was spent on homework?

What facts can you gather from the circle graph?

$\frac{3}{8}$ sleeping; $\frac{1}{3}$ at school; $\frac{1}{6}$ free time; $\frac{1}{8}$ on homework.

Which of the facts from the circle graph are important for solving the problem?

Lauren spends $\frac{1}{8}$ of her Monday on homework.

PLAN

What operation should you choose to solve the problem?

multiplication

SOLVE

What is the solution?

$\frac{1}{16}$

LOOK BACK

What operation could you use to check your answer? Explain.

Possible Answer: You could use division to check your answer. $\frac{1}{16} \div \frac{1}{2} = \frac{1}{8}$

Choose the correct operation. Then solve.

2. What part of her day did Lauren spend at school or doing homework? Was it more or less than half the day?

addition; $\frac{11}{24}$; less than $\frac{1}{2}$

Copyright © Houghton Mifflin Company. All rights reserved.

Use with text pages 328–329.

Explore Multiplication

Show Your Work

1. Lori's team won 0.7 of their games. They won half their games by 10 or more points. What decimal describes how many games Lori's team won by 10 or more points?

0.35 of their games

2. Lori's team lost 0.3 of their games. The team lost $\frac{2}{5}$ of those games by 5. What decimal describes how many games Lori's team lost by 5 points?

0.12 of their games

3. During a game, Lori usually drinks 1.5 liters of water. In her last game, Lori only drank 0.8 of that amount. How many liters of water did Lori drink?

1.2 liters

4. Neil said that $0.6 \times 0.7 = 0.7 \times 0.6$. Is he right? Explain your answer.

Yes; *Possible answer:* The Commutative Property of Multiplication works for decimals.

5. Will multiplying two decimals less than 1 always result in a product less than 1? Explain your thinking.

Yes; *Possible answer:* Since $1 \times 1 = 1$, multiplying two decimals less than 1 will result in a product less than 1.

Copyright © Houghton Mifflin Company. All rights reserved.

Use with text pages 334–335.

Multiply Whole Numbers and Decimals

Use the data in the table to solve Problems 1–5.

Show Your Work

1. Mark was recently promoted to manager of The Sub Shop, and received a raise of $1.50 per hour. If he worked the same number of hours before the promotion, how much more will he make per week?

   _____ $60 per week _____

The Sub Shop		
Employee	**Hours Per Week**	**Pay Per Hour**
Rosa	32	$8.60
Shing	25	$9.20
Maryann	36	$9.60
Mark	40	$12.50

2. Overtime pay is 1.5 times an employee's normal pay. How much money would Maryann make per hour if she works overtime?

   _____ $14.40 per hour _____

3. Who makes more money per week, Rosa or Shing? Explain.

   Rosa; *Possible answer:*
   Rosa makes $275.20 per week and Shing
   makes $230 per week, $275.20 > $230.

   4. $132.53; *Possible answer:* $132.525 has to
   be rounded to the nearest cent, since there
   are 3 decimal places
   in the product and
   money only goes to
   2 decimal places.

4. Suppose that The Sub Shop hired another employee who worked 15.5 hours each week for $8.55 per hour. What would this employee's weekly pay be? Explain.

   _____

   5. 8 hours at normal pay; 6 hours at overtime
   pay; *Possible answer:* If Shing works 8 hours
   at normal pay, he will
   bring home $303.60.
   If he works 6 hours at
   overtime pay, he will
   bring home $312.80.

5. Shing wants to earn $300 next week. He has agreed to work extra hours. How many extra hours will he have to work at normal pay to reach his goal? How many extra hours will he have to work at overtime pay to reach his goal? Explain your answers.

   _____

Copyright © Houghton Mifflin Company. All rights reserved.

Name _____ Date _____

Estimate Products

1-5: *Estimates may vary.*

Show Your Work

1. Suppose the exchange rate for Russian rubles to U.S. dollars is about 31.735 rubles for every dollar. If a tourist exchanges $28, about how many rubles will she get?

   about 900 rubles

2. Suppose the Canadian dollar is worth about $0.64 U.S. About how much is $90 Canadian worth in U.S. dollars? What fraction could you use for your estimate?

   $60 U.S.; $\frac{2}{3}$

3. Suppose one U.S. dollar is worth about 48.35 Indian rupees. Liam said that $20 U.S. are worth about 100 rupees. Explain what Liam's mistake was. Then tell the correct estimate.

   Liam rounded the number of rupees to 50, but then multiplied by 2 instead of by 20; about 1,000 rupees

4. Linda is visiting Sweden. Linda exchanges $82 for the krona, Sweden's currency. If each U.S. dollar is worth 9.323 krona; about how many krona does Linda receive?

   about 800 krona

5. Christina said that 58 × 0.78 is about 45. Robbie said that 58 × 0.78 is about 48. Who is correct? Explain your thinking.

   Both are correct; Christina rounded 58 to 60 and 0.78 to $\frac{3}{4}$: 60 × $\frac{3}{4}$ = 45. Robbie rounded 58 to 60 and 0.78 to 0.8: 60 × 0.8 = 48.

Copyright © Houghton Mifflin Company. All rights reserved.

Use with text pages 338–339.

Multiply Decimals

Show Your Work

1. August is the wettest month of the year in Miami, Florida. Miami receives an average of 8.63 inches of rain each August. If it only rains 0.8 of the average amount next August, how much rain will Miami get?

   6.904 inches

2. Phoenix, Arizona, is one of the driest cities in the United States. It receives just 8.29 inches of rain each year. If Phoenix receives the same amount of rain each month, how much rain will it get in 1.5 years?

   12.44 inches

3. Duluth, Minnesota, has a mean yearly precipitation of 31 inches. San Diego, California, has a mean yearly precipitation that is 0.345 of Duluth's. What is San Diego's mean yearly precipitation?

   10.695 inches

4. Indianapolis, Indiana, receives an average of 40.95 inches of precipitation each year. To find the mean precipitation for one fourth of the year in Indianapolis, would you multiply by 0.25 or by $\frac{1}{4}$? Explain.

   Possible answer: It is easier to multiply by 0.25 to find the exact answer.

5. If you multiply 0.73 by 2.52, how many decimal places will be in the product? How do you know? 4; Each factor has 2 decimal places and 2 + 2 = 4.

Copyright © Houghton Mifflin Company. All rights reserved.

Use with text pages 340–342.

Zeros in the Product

Show Your Work

1. The disk-winged bat is found in Central and South America. It weighs 0.14 ounce. The Kitti's hognosed bat weighs 0.5 of the disk-winged bat. How many ounces does the Kitti's hognosed bat weigh?

   _____ 0.07 ounce _____

2. The California myotis bat weighs 0.18 ounce. The banana bat, from Africa, is about 0.61 the weight of the California myotis. What is the weight of the banana bat?

   _____ 0.1098 ounce _____

3. Offensive linemen in the National Football League often weigh 0.16 of a ton. If you weigh 0.25 of a lineman's weight, what part of a ton do you weigh?

   _____ 0.04 ton _____

4. Manesh wrote that 0.2 × 0.02 = 0.04. Explain what Manesh's mistake was. Then tell the correct answer.

   Possible answer: The multipliers have a total of 3 decimal places and Manesh's product only has 2 decimal places.

5. Odessa said the product of 0.04 and 0.25 will have 4 decimal places. Floyd said that the product will have 2 decimal places. Who is correct? Explain.

   Possible answer: They are both correct; 0.04 × 0.25 = 0.0100, which simplifies to 0.01.

Copyright © Houghton Mifflin Company. All rights reserved.

Use with text pages 344–345.

Problem-Solving Decision:
Reasonable Answers

1. To pay his first month's rent, Kevin uses 0.4 of his take-home pay. His take-home pay is $1,200 each month. Kevin says his rent is $400. Is Kevin correct?

UNDERSTAND

What does the question ask?

Is Kevin's rent $400 each month?

What information do you know?

Kevin pays 0.4 of $1,200 each month.

PLAN

Which operation do you need to use to find Kevin's rent?

multiplication

SOLVE

How much is Kevin's rent each month?

$1,200 × 0.4 = $480

Is Kevin correct?

No

If he is not correct, how much money was he wrong by?

$80

LOOK BACK

How can you check that your answer is reasonable?

$\frac{400}{1,200} = \frac{1}{3} = 0.3$, which is less than 0.4. Since Kevin thought his rent was less than it really was, the answer is reasonable.

Solve the problem to determine if the answer is reasonable.

2. There are 20 teabags in each box of the tea Barbara bought last week. Barbara said she used 0.75 of one of the boxes to make iced tea. There were 5 teabags left. Was Barbara correct?

Yes; 20 × 0.75 = 15. She used 15 teabags and had 5 left.

Copyright © Houghton Mifflin Company. All rights reserved.

Use with text pages 346–347.

Name _____ Date _____

Explore Division With Decimals

Show Your Work

1. Radio station WXYZ gives away a prize every 0.5 hour between 3 P.M. and 7 P.M. How many prizes does the station give away during that time?

_____8 prizes_____

2. The station identifies itself every 0.8 hour. How many times does the station identify itself during an 8-hour period?

_____10 times_____

3. WXYZ is sponsoring a 5-kilometer run for charity. They plan to display a station banner every 0.2 kilometer. How many banners will the station display?

_____25 banners_____

4. When the disc jockey says a special word, a listener can call to win a prize. If the disc jockey uses that word every 0.25 hour, how many listeners can win a prize during a 4-hour shift?

16 listeners can win

5. The station gives away $1,000 every 0.4 month. The disc jockey says that the station gives away money 300 times a year. Is the disc jockey's number reasonable? Explain.

No; Possible explanation: 12 ÷ 0.4 = 30, so the station gives away $1,000 thirty times each year.

Copyright © Houghton Mifflin Company. All rights reserved.

Use with text pages 352–353.

Estimate Quotients

1–4: *Estimates may vary.*

Show Your Work

1. Batting averages are determined by the number of hits divided by the number of at bats. If Samantha has a batting average of 0.481 with 38 hits, about how many at bats does she have?

   _____80 at bats_____

2. A baseball team won 0.383 of its games in 2002. The team won 62 games. About how many games did the team play?

   _____160 games_____

3. The team's right fielder had a batting average of 0.251 in 2002. He had 121 hits. About how many at bats did he have?

   _____480 at bats_____

4. If a team won 0.225 of its games and won 8 games, estimate the number of games the team played.

   _____36 games_____

5. Ted Williams was the last batter to hit over 0.400 for a full season. He hit 0.406 in 1941. Which equivalent unit fraction would you use to estimate the number of at bats Williams had, if you were given his total number of hits? Explain.

   which is equal to $\frac{1}{5} + \frac{1}{5}$ or $\frac{2}{5}$. I would use $\frac{1}{3}$ since $\frac{2}{5}$ is closer to $\frac{1}{3}$

   Possible explanation: 0.406 is close to 0.400, than it is to $\frac{1}{2}$.

Copyright © Houghton Mifflin Company. All rights reserved.

Use with text pages 354–355.

Name _____   Date _____

Multiply and Divide
by Powers of 10

Show Your Work

1. New York's Verrazano Narrows Bridge
is the longest suspension bridge in the
United States. It is 4.26×10^3 feet long.
How long is it?

_____4,260 feet_____

2. The George Washington Bridge that
connects New York and New Jersey
is 7.6×10^2 feet shorter than the
Verrazano Narrows Bridge. Use the
information in Problem 1 to find the
length of the George Washington Bridge.

_____3,500 feet_____

3. New York's Arthur Kill Bridge is the
longest drawbridge in the United States.
The bridge is $5,580 \div 10^1$ feet long.
How long is the bridge?

_____558 feet_____

4. The Golden Gate Bridge in San Francisco
is 1,280 meters long. To find its length in
kilometers, should you multiply by 10^3 or
divide by 10^3? Explain. Possible answer: divide
by 10^3; divide to change smaller units into
larger units: 1,000 meters = 1 kilometer

5. The Greater New Orleans Bridge is the
longest cantilever bridge in the United
States. Its length is 1,575 feet. Write a
question about the bridge and use a
power of 10 in the answer.
Possible explanation: How can you use a
power of 10 to describe how long the
Greater New Orleans Bridge is in feet?
$1,575 \times 10^3$

Copyright © Houghton Mifflin Company. All rights reserved.

Use with text pages 356–357.

Divide a Decimal by a Whole Number

Show Your Work

1. Mary is training for a 10-kilometer race.
She runs 65.1 kilometers each week. If
she runs 7 days each week and she runs
the same distance each day, how many
kilometers does she run each day?

_____9.3 kilometers_____

2. Suppose that Mary does not run on
Sunday and runs 64.8 kilometers per
week. How many kilometers does she
run each day if she continues to
run the same distance each day?

_____10.8 kilometers_____

3. Dan is running a 6-hour race. Whoever
runs the farthest distance in 6 hours is
the winner. Dan's goal is to run 45.6
miles during that time. How many
miles should he run each hour to
reach his goal?

_____7.6 miles each hour_____

4. An Olympic runner can run a mile in
about 3.92 minutes. It takes 4 laps
around an Olympic track to run a mile. If
the runner runs at the same speed for
each lap, how many minutes does it take
the runner to run one lap?

_____0.98 minute_____

5. John wants to run a marathon, which is
26.2 miles. He said if he can run 7 miles
each hour, he can complete the race in
under 4 hours. Is he correct? Explain.

Yes; Possible explanation: If he runs
7 miles each hour, he can run 26.2 miles
in about 3.7 hours.

Copyright © Houghton Mifflin Company. All rights reserved.

Use with text pages 358–360.

Write Zeros in the Dividend

Show Your Work

1. Dr. Travis saw 32 patients last week at her office. If she worked 5 days last week, what is the mean number of patients she saw each day?

_____ 6.4 patients _____

2. Suppose that 20 of Dr. Travis's patients needed a note to excuse them from school. What part of all her patients last week needed a doctor's note?

0.625 of her patients

3. Dr. Travis saw 25, 38, 28, and 31 patients each week for the past 4 weeks. What is the mean number of patients she saw each week?

_____ 30.5 patients _____

4. Part of Dr. Travis's job is to see patients in the hospital. She visited the hospital 158 times in the last 8 months. What is the mean number of times Dr. Travis visited the hospital each month?

19.75 times per month

5. Dr. Travis worked 5 days last week and was at her office for 45.3 hours last week. Gwen wrote that Dr. Travis worked an average of 9.6 hours per day. Explain Gwen's mistake. Then tell the correct answer.

Gwen forgot to write a zero in the tenths place of the quotient; 9.06 hours per day.

Copyright © Houghton Mifflin Company. All rights reserved.

Use with text pages 362–364.

Repeating Decimals

Show Your Work

1. In basketball, a shooting average is calculated by dividing the number of shots
made by the number of shots attempted.
In her last game Kristen took 18 shots
and made 12. Write her shooting
average as a repeating decimal.

_____ 0.6 _____

2. In many sports, averages are calculated
to the thousandths place regardless of
whether the decimal repeats. What place
do you need to divide to in order to
round a decimal in the thousandths
place?

ten thousandths place

3. Use the information in Problem 1 to find
Kristen's shooting average rounded to
the nearest thousandth.

_____ 0.667 _____

4. Kristen has made 22 free throws and
missed 6 this season. What part of all
her free throws has she made? Write
your answer as a repeating decimal.

_____ 0.78571428 _____

5. Can a decimal greater than 1 be a
repeating decimal? Explain why or
why not.

Yes; *Possible explanation:* Any number
that is not a multiple of 3 that is divided
by 3 will be a repeating decimal.

Copyright © Houghton Mifflin Company. All rights reserved.

Use with text pages 366–367.

Divide a Decimal by a Decimal

Show Your Work

1. The Indianapolis 500 is a 500-mile car race. Each lap of the Indianapolis 500 is 2.5 miles. How many laps does each driver need to drive to finish the race?

   _____200 laps_____

2. Each lap of a running track is 0.25 kilometer. How many laps will a runner need to run in order to run 3.2 kilometers?

   _____12.8 laps_____

3. Darren plans to hike 27.2 miles in January. If he hikes 3.4 miles each time he hikes, how many times does he plan to hike in January?

   _____8 times_____

5. Possible answer: The divisor has to be changed to a whole number by multiplying it by a power of 10 and then multiplying the dividend by the same power of 10. They are the same in that the decimal point in quotient is placed above the decimal point in the dividend and zeros are added after the decimal in dividend to continue dividing.

4. To reach the hiking trails, Darren drives 75 miles. His pickup truck gets 13.6 miles per gallon. Rounded to the nearest tenth of a gallon, how many gallons did Darren use?

   _____5.5 gallons_____

5. How is dividing by decimal divisors different than dividing by whole number divisors? How is it the same?

   _____

   _____

   _____

Copyright © Houghton Mifflin Company. All rights reserved.

Use with text pages 368–369.

Problem-Solving Application: Decide
How to Write the Quotient

1. Ms. Brown's class is going to Orlando, Florida,
for a class trip. It costs $4,818 to send 24 students.
How much does it cost per student?

UNDERSTAND

What is the question?

How much will the trip cost per student?

What do you know?

The cost for 24 students.

What operation do you need to use?

division

PLAN

Decide how to write the quotient to solve the
problem. Will you write the quotient as a fraction Since the problem
or as a decimal?
involves money, the quotient will be a decimal.

SOLVE

What is the solution to the problem?

$200.75

LOOK BACK

How can you check your answer?

$200.75 × 24 = $4,818

2. The class made 2 trips to a water park. If they spent
9 hours total at the water park, how many hours did
they spend per trip?

$9 \div 2 = 4\frac{1}{2}$ or 4.5. The answer
can be either a fraction or a
decimal.

Copyright © Houghton Mifflin Company. All rights reserved.

Use with text pages 370–372.

Points, Lines, and Rays

Show Your Work

1. Draw an outline of your classroom. Which of the following are in your drawing: point, line, line segment, ray, or plane?

   Possible answer: points, line segments, and plane.

2. How many rectangles are there when 4 parallel lines are perpendicular to 3 parallel lines?

   6 rectangles

3. Michele said that the figure should be labeled $\overrightarrow{FE}$. Explain what Michele's mistake was. Then tell the correct answer.

   Michele mixed up the order of the points; $\overrightarrow{EF}$.

4. Name one line segment and one ray that can be found in the diagram.

   Possible answer: $\overline{AB}$ and $\overrightarrow{AB}$.

5. Marco said that all perpendicular lines are intersecting lines, but not all intersecting lines are perpendicular. Is he correct? Explain.

   Yes; *Possible answer:* only intersecting lines that intersect at right angles are perpendicular lines.

Copyright © Houghton Mifflin Company. All rights reserved.

Use with text pages 390–391.

Name _____ Date _____

Measure, Draw, and Classify Angles

Show Your Work

1. If a right angle is split in half, how can the two new angles be classified? What is the measure of each angle?

    2 acute angles; 45°

2. If an obtuse angle is split in half, how can the two new angles be classified? Give an example.

    2 acute angles;
    Possible answer:

    a 160° angle split in half will
    form two 80° angles

3. Karen said that perpendicular lines form 2 right angles. Dexter thinks Karen meant 4 right angles. Who is correct? Draw an example.

    Dexter is correct

    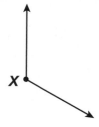

4. Marie measured the angle as 60°. Explain what Marie's mistake was. What is the correct measure of this angle?

    Possible answer:
    Marie used the wrong part of the protractor to measure the angle. The measure of the angle is 120°.

    X

5. Which is greater, the measure of a straight angle and an acute angle, or the measure of two obtuse angles? Explain.

    Either; Possible answer:
    A straight angle plus an acute angle is greater than 180° and less than 270°. Two obtuse angles are greater than 180° and less than 360°.

Copyright © Houghton Mifflin Company. All rights reserved.

Use with text pages 392–395.

Triangles

Show Your Work

1. Mavis has found the measures of two angles of a triangle: 72° and 47°. Without measuring, how can she find the measure of the third angle? What is the measure of the third angle?

Subtract the sum of 72 and 47 from 180; 61°

_____

2. Kan measured the angles of an isosceles triangle. One angle measure is 36°. The other two angles have the same measure. What is the measure of each of the two other angles?

72°

_____

3. What triangles are formed when you draw a line down the middle of an equilateral triangle?

two right triangles

_____

4. Use the clues to find the angle measures of the following triangle:
   • The second angle is double the measure of the first angle.
   • The third angle is the sum of the other two angle measures.

30°, 60°, and 90°

_____

5. Can the measure of an angle in an equilateral triangle be anything other than 60°? Explain. No; *Possible answer: Since all the sides are the same length, all the angles are equal, and 180° ÷ 3 = 60°.*

Copyright © Houghton Mifflin Company. All rights reserved.

Use with text pages 396–397.

Congruence

1. Which parts of the United States flag are congruent?

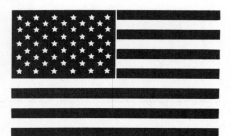

Show Your Work

6 long stripes, 7 short stripes, and the 50 stars

2. Do any parts of the flags of Australia and New Zealand appear to be congruent? Explain.

The upper left-hand corners of the flags are congruent.

3. Chris said that the only triangle that has all congruent sides and angles is an isosceles right triangle. Explain what Chris's mistake was.

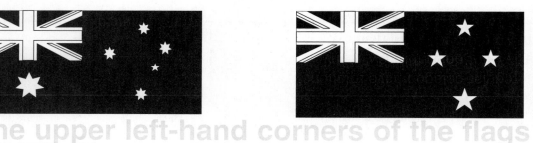

Possible answer: An isosceles right triangle has two congruent sides and angles, but one side and angle are not congruent.

4. Mr. Hopkins drew a square that was 4.5 inches on each side. He then drew a square that was 4.52 inches on each side. Are the squares congruent? Explain.

No; To be congruent, the sides must be the same length.

Copyright © Houghton Mifflin Company. All rights reserved.

Quadrilaterals and Other Polygons

Show Your Work

1. Which polygons are on the United States flag?

rectangles and decagons

2. What three polygons are on the flag of the Bahamas?

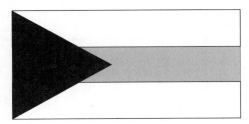

Bahamas flag

triangle, trapezoid, pentagon

3. When can a rectangle also be a rhombus? Explain.

Possible answer: When the rectangle is a square. A square fits the definition of a rhombus.

4. Three angles of a quadrilateral have measures of 107°, 83°, and 75°. What is the measure of the fourth angle?

95°

5. All squares are rectangles, but are all rectangles squares? Explain why or why not.

No; Possible answer: only rectangles with 4 congruent sides are squares.

Copyright © Houghton Mifflin Company. All rights reserved.

Use with text pages 400–402.

Rotations, Reflections, and Translations

a b c d e f g h i j k l m n o p q r s t u v w x y z
A B C D E F G H I J K L M N O P Q R S T U V W X Y Z

Show Your Work

1. Which lower-case letters of the alphabet can be transformed to create different letters?

b, d, n, u

2. Find two lower-case letters that are transformations of the letter **b**.

d, p

3. Look at the reflection of the letter **A** across a vertical line: **A | A**. It is unchanged. Which other capital letters will remain unchanged by a reflection across a vertical line?

H, I, M, O, T, U, V, W, X, Y

4. Simone drew two congruent triangles. Triangle C is 2 inches lower on the page than triangle D. What type of transformation has Simone made?

translation

5. Jimmy rotated and translated a triangle. He said the rotated and translated triangle was congruent to the original triangle. Is he correct? Explain.

Yes; Possible answer: A transformation changes the location of a figure, not its size or shape.

Copyright © Houghton Mifflin Company. All rights reserved.

Use with text pages 404–406.

Problem-Solving Strategy:
Make a Model

Make a model to solve the following problems.

1. Mrs. Dolan wants to tile her kitchen floor with tiles in the shape of regular pentagons. Will regular pentagons tessellate?

UNDERSTAND

What is the question?

Will regular pentagons tessellate?

What do you know about tessellations?

A tessellation is a repeating pattern that covers a plane without gaps or overlaps.

PLAN

Make models of congruent regular pentagons.

Check models.

SOLVE

Use translations to fit the regular pentagons together. Do they fit without gaps or overlaps?

No.

LOOK BACK

Does your answer make sense?

Yes; Possible answer: I cannot tile regular pentagons without gaps or overlaps.

2. Mrs. Dolan decides to try tiling her kitchen with congrugent isosceles right triangle tiles. Will congruent isosceles right triangles tessalate? Explain.

Yes; Possible answer: Any set of congruent triangles will tessellate.

Copyright © Houghton Mifflin Company. All rights reserved.

Use with text pages 408–410.

Name _____ Date _____

Circles

Show Your Work

1. When a clock reads 3:00, one of the angles formed by the minute hand and the hour hand is 90°. What is the measure of the other angle?

   _____270°_____

2. Carlos drew the circle below. He said that the diameter is $\overline{MN}$. Is he correct? Explain why or why not.

   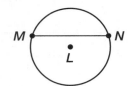

   _____

   No; *Possible answer:* A diameter must pass through the center of the circle. $\overline{MN}$ is a chord.

3. Ramona said that there is an infinite number of central angles in a circle. Is she correct? Explain why or why not.

   Yes; *Possible answer:* Any angle with its vertex at the center of the circle is a central angle.

4. Can you draw a circle if you know only the measure of a chord that is not a diameter? Explain why or why not.

   No; *Possible answer:* You need to know the length of a radius or diameter to draw a circle.

5. A full turn of 360° is not used to describe rotational symmetry. Why not?

   Possible answer: A turn of 360° results in the original figure.

Copyright © Houghton Mifflin Company. All rights reserved.

Use with text pages 412–413.

Symmetry

ABCDEFGHIJKLMNOPQRSTUVWXYZ

Show Your Work

1. Which upper-case letters of the alphabet have line symmetry?

A, B, C, D, E, H, I, M, N, O, T, U, V, W, X

2. Which upper-case letters of the alphabet have rotational symmetry?

H, I, N, O, S, X, Z

3. Does a regular octagon have rotational symmetry? If it does, tell how many degrees you turned it.

Yes; Possible answer: 180°.

4. An equilateral triangle has 3 lines of symmetry. A square has 4 lines of symmetry. A regular pentagon has 5 lines of symmetry. How many lines of symmetry will a regular hexagon have?

6 lines of symmetry

5. A full turn of 360° is not used to describe rotational symmetry. Why not?

Possible answer: A turn of 360° results in the original figure.

Copyright © Houghton Mifflin Company. All rights reserved.

Use with text pages 414–416.

Perimeter

Show Your Work

1. Ryan wants to put a fence around a
rectangular dog run with a length of
20 meters and a width of 12 meters. How
many meters of fence does Ryan need?

___64 meters___

2. Suppose that Ryan wants to build another
dog run $\frac{1}{2}$ the length of the first one.
What is the new perimeter?

___44 meters___

3. Ryan's mother has a fenced rectangular garden that measures 15 meters $\times$ 10 meters.
One of the 10-meter sides is along the house
and doesn't have a fence. How many meters
of fence border the garden?

___40 meters___

4. Use whole numbers to find how many
different rectangles have a perimeter
of 20 units. What are the dimensions
of these rectangles?

5; 1 $\times$ 9, 2 $\times$ 8,
3 $\times$ 7, 4 $\times$ 6,
5 $\times$ 5

5. How does the perimeter of a figure
change if the dimensions are changed
from yards to feet? Give an example.

5. Possible answer:
The perimeter remains the
same, but the units are
multiplied by 3 since 1 yard
= 3 feet; A rectangle with a length of 2 yards and
a width of 1 yard has a perimeter of 6 yards. That
same rectangle has a length of 6 feet and a
width of 3 feet and a perimeter of 18 feet.

Copyright © Houghton Mifflin Company. All rights reserved.

Use with text pages 422–423.

Problem-Solving Strategy:
Find a Pattern

1. Find a pattern in the designs. How many squares
will there be in the eighth design of your pattern?

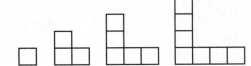

UNDERSTAND

What does the question ask? *How many squares will there be in the eighth design of your pattern?*

What do you know? *There are 4 designs.*

How many squares are in each design? *1 square, 3 squares, 5 squares, 7 squares.*

PLAN

Look at the numbers in this pattern. Do they
seem to increase by addition or multiplication? *Addition*

SOLVE

What is the pattern of the design? *The design adds 1 square to the top and to the right of the previous design.*

How many squares are added with each design? *Each design has 2 more squares than the one before it.*

How many squares will be in the eighth design? *There will be 15 squares in the eighth design.*

LOOK BACK

Draw the eighth design to check your answer. *Check drawings. The drawing should be a L-shaped with 8 squares up and 8 squares across at the bottom.*

Find a pattern to help solve the following problem.

$2^1 = 2$, $2^2 = 4$, $2^3 = 8$, $2^4 = 16$, $2^5 = 32$.

2. What is the ones digit of 2^{25}? *2^{25} will have a ones digit of 2.*

Copyright © Houghton Mifflin Company. All rights reserved.

Use with text pages 424–426.

Area of a Parallelogram

Show Your Work

1. The dimensions of Stephanie's rectangular bedroom are 16 feet × 13 feet. What
   is the area of her bedroom?

   __208 square feet__

2. Gopal's living room is shaped like a
   square and its area is 225 square feet.
   What is the length of each side?

   __15 feet__

3. Paulina said that two parallelograms with
   different shapes can have the same area.
   Is she correct? Give an example.

   Yes; Possible answer:
   A parallelogram with
   a base of 10 units and a
   height of 4 units has an area
   of 40 square units, and a parallelogram with a
   base of 8 units and a height of 5 units also
   has an area of 40 square units.

4. What happens to the perimeter of a
   square when the dimensions are tripled?

   the perimeter
   is multiplied by 3

5. Can two rectangles have the same
   perimeter but different areas? Give
   an example.

   Yes; Possible answer:
   a rectangle with dimensions
   of 10 units × 2 units has a
   perimeter of 24 units and an
   area of 20 square units and a rectangle with
   dimensions of 7 units × 5 units has a perimeter of 24 units and an area of 35 square units.

Copyright © Houghton Mifflin Company. All rights reserved.

Use with text pages 428–430.

Area of a Triangle

Find the area of each triangle.

Show Your Work

1. The teachers at Jefferson Elementary handed out triangle-shaped pennants on the first day of school. If each pennant has a base of 5 inches and a height of 12 inches, what is the area of each pennant?

   30 square inches

2. At football games, the local high school sells large pennants. If each pennant has a base of 1 foot and a height of 2.5 feet, what is the area of each pennant in square inches?

   180 square inches

3. Suppose that the high school also sells a small pennant. If the small pennant has a height of 24 inches and the area is 108 square inches, what is the length of the base of the pennant?

   9 inches

4. How are the area formulas of triangles and parallelograms alike? How are they different?

   Possible answer: To find the area of both, it is necessary to multiply the base times the height. For the area of a triangle, it is also necessary to multiply by $\frac{1}{2}$.

5. A triangle has a base of 8 feet and a height of 6 feet. Beatrix says the area of the triangle is 48 square feet. Explain what Beatrix's mistake was. Then tell the correct answer.

   Possible answer: Beatrix forgot to multiply the base times the height by $\frac{1}{2}$; 24 square feet

Copyright © Houghton Mifflin Company. All rights reserved.

Use with text pages 432–433.

Perimeter and Area of Irregular Figures

1. Mr. Momary told his class to find the area of the H on the field of Haines Elementary School. Use the dimensions in the figure to find the area.

   <u>_____72 square feet_____</u>

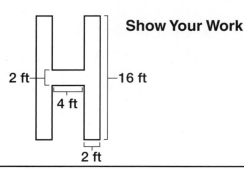

Show Your Work

2 ft —| |— 16 ft

4 ft

2 ft

2. What is the perimeter of the H in Problem 1?

   <u>_____76 feet_____</u>

3. North Park is 60 yards × 25 yards. The park has a blacktop playground of 20 yards by 15 yards and the rest is grass. What is the area of the grass?

   <u>_____1,200 square yards_____</u>

4. Draw an irregular figure on grid paper. Then find the area and perimeter of your figure.

   Check drawings and answers.

   Possible answer:

5. Estimate the area of the figure. How did you find your answer?

   About 27 square units; Find the number of whole squares and then the partial squares. Then estimate the number of partial squares that can be combined to make a whole square. Then add the numbers.

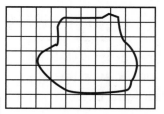

Copyright © Houghton Mifflin Company. All rights reserved.

Use with text pages 434–436.

Name _____ Date _____

Circumference of a Circle

Show Your Work

1. A dog toy has a radius of 6 inches. What is its circumference? Use 3.14 for π. Round your answer to the nearest inch.

   _____38 inches_____

2. The diameter of a container of blank CDs is $4\frac{5}{6}$ inches. What is its circumference? Use $\frac{22}{7}$ for π.

   _____$15\frac{4}{21}$ inches_____

3. Paul measured a circle with a radius of 4 inches. He said the circumference is 12.56 inches. Explain what Paul's mistake was. Then tell the correct answer.

   Paul forgot to multiply the radius by 2; 25.12

4. Lee's coffee mug has a diameter of 7.5 centimeters. What is the circumference of the coffee mug? Use 3.14 for π. Round your answer to the nearest tenth.

   _____23.6 centimeters_____

5. If you know the circumference of a circle, how can you find the diameter?

   You can divide the circumference by $\frac{22}{7}$ or 3.14 to find the diameter.

Copyright © Houghton Mifflin Company. All rights reserved.

Use with text pages 438–440.

Name _____ Date _____

Solid Figures

Show Your Work

1. The Grand Louvre, the main entrance to the Louvre Museum in Paris, France, has a square base and 5 faces, 8 edges, and 5 vertices. Which solid figure is it?

   __square pyramid__

2. The Renaissance Center in Detroit, Michigan, has 2 circular bases in its design. Which solid figure is it?

   __cylinder__

3. Two girls are playing sports. Leanne is playing with a cylinder, and Samantha is playing with a sphere. Each girl is playing either basketball or hockey. Who is playing which sport? Explain.

   __Leanne is playing hockey because a hockey puck is a cylinder; Samantha is playing basketball because a basketball is a sphere.__

4. How many different solid figures are in your classroom? List them.

   __Check answers.__

5. Leon says that all cubes are rectangular prisms and all rectangular prisms are cubes. Is Leon correct? Explain.

   __No; Possible explanation: All cubes are rectangular prisms, but a rectangular prism is a cube only when it has 6 square faces.__

Copyright © Houghton Mifflin Company. All rights reserved.

Use with text pages 446–447.

Two-Dimensional Views of Solid Figures

Show Your Work

1. Sketch a front, top, and right-side view of the figure.

front   top   side

---

2. Which solid figure has the same view from the top, the side, and the front?

Answers will vary.
Possible answers:
cube or sphere

---

3. Draw the figure using these views.

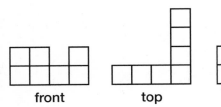

front   top   right

Possible answer:

---

4. Sketch the front, top, and side view of a figure. Give it to a classmate to build.

Check drawings.

---

5. Why can you only see part of a solid figure from the top, front, or side?

Possible answer: If you are looking from one side, the other side is hidden. If you are looking from the top, the bottom is hidden. If you are looking from the front, the back is hidden.

Copyright © Houghton Mifflin Company. All rights reserved.

Use with text pages 448–449.

Name _____ Date _____

Nets

Show Your Work

1. A net has 4 large rectangles and
2 small rectangles. Which solid
figure will it make?

rectangular prism

2. Ellis drew this net for a cube.

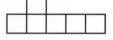

Ellis misplaced one square; Line up 4
squares in a row. Add a square above

Explain his mistake. Then tell what the
net should look like.

and below the second
square from the left.

3. What shape will this net form?

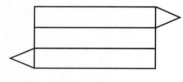

triangular prism

4. Draw the net of a cereal box.

5. Explain how to make a net for a
square pyramid.

Possible answer: First draw a square. Then
draw 4 equilateral triangles, one on each
side of the square.

Copyright © Houghton Mifflin Company. All rights reserved.

Use with text pages 450–451.

Name _____   Date _____

Surface Area

Show Your Work

1. For his birthday Jerry received a box that was 15 inches long, 8 inches wide, and 3 inches high. What is the surface area of the box?

   _____378 in.²_____

2. Jerry also got a present in a box 12 inches long, 7.5 inches wide, and 6 inches high. Is the surface area of this box greater than or less than the surface area of the box in Problem 1? By how much?

   _____

   The second box has a surface area of 414 in.², so it is 36 in.² larger than the box in Problem 1.

3. How can you find the surface area of a cube without measuring each face?

   Find the area of one face and multiply by 6.

4. Find the surface area of your math book.

   Check answers.

5. A box measures 10.1 centimeters × 10.5 centimeters × 10.3 centimeters. Will 600 square centimeters of wrapping paper cover the surface of the box? Explain.

   No; Possible explanation: A 10 cm × 10 cm × 10 cm box has a surface area of 600 cm². Since each dimension of the box is greater than 10 cm, the surface area will be greater than 600 cm².

Copyright © Houghton Mifflin Company. All rights reserved.

Use with text pages 452–454.

Problem-Solving Strategy: Solve a Simpler Problem

1. There are 32 schools that participated in a statewide trivia tournament. In each round, one school played one match against another school and the winner continued on until 1 school remained. How many total matches were played?

UNDERSTAND

What is the question?
How many games?

What information do you know?
32 compete. 1 school wins.

PLAN

Could solving a simpler problem help you to solve the original problem?
Yes.

SOLVE

How many matches are there in the first round?
How many schools are left for the second round?
16 games; 16 schools

Solve the problem.
31 matches

LOOK BACK

Is your answer reasonable?
Yes; 1 total game less than teams.

Solve.

2. A restaurant has 24 tables that each can sit 2 people per side. If the tables are pushed together for a banquet, how many people can sit at the table?

100

Copyright © Houghton Mifflin Company. All rights reserved.

Use with text pages 456–458.

Name _____ Date _____

Volume

Show Your Work

1. Billy has a rectangular fish tank that is
   2 feet × 1.5 feet × 0.6 foot. What is the
   volume of the fish tank?

   _____ 1.8 ft³ _____

2. A rectangular swimming pool has a
   length of 50 meters, a width of 25
   meters, and had an average depth
   of 3 meters. What is the volume of
   the pool?

   _____ 3,750 m³ _____

3. Suppose that the swimming pool in
   Problem 2 had an average depth of
   1.5 meters for 30 meters of the length
   and an average depth of 3 meters for
   20 meters of the length. How much less
   volume would the pool have?

   _____ 1,125 m³ _____

4. A cubic centimeter holds 1 milliliter of
   water. Find the capacity of water in liters
   that this triangular prism holds.

   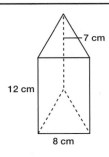

   7 cm

   12 cm

   8 cm

   _____ 0.336 L _____

5. What happens to the volume of a cube if
   you double its length? Give an example.

   Possible answer: the volume is increased
   8 times; a cube that is 2 cm in length has
   a volume of 8 cm³ and a cube that is 4 cm
   in length has a volume of 64 cm³.

Copyright © Houghton Mifflin Company. All rights reserved.

Use with text pages 460–463.

Problem-Solving Strategy:
Use Formulas

1. Nate installs 324 square feet of carpet in a house.
The room is 18 feet long. What is the width of the room?

UNDERSTAND

What is the question?

<u>What is the width of the room?</u>

What information do you know? The area is 324 ft² and
the length of the room is 18 ft.

PLAN

Which formula can you use to find the width
of the room?

<u>A = l × w</u>

SOLVE

Find the width of the room.

<u>324 = 18 × w; w = 18</u>

What shape is the room?

<u>The room is an 18-foot square.</u>

LOOK BACK

How can you check your answer?

<u>324 ÷ 18 = 18</u>

Solve.

2. Store It Yourself offers a stall with 2,000 cubic feet of storage for a low price.
The ceilings are 8 feet high and the width of the stall is 10 feet. What is the
length of the stall?

<u>The length is 25 feet.</u>

Copyright © Houghton Mifflin Company. All rights reserved.

Use with text pages 464–466.

Name _____ Date _____

Ratios

Write each ratio three different ways.

Show Your Work

1. Hector has a dollar's worth of quarters and a dollar's worth of dimes. What is the ratio of quarters to dimes?

   4 to 10; 4:10; $\frac{4}{10}$

2. Hector also has a dollar's worth of half dollars. What is the ratio of quarters to half dollars?

   4 to 2; 4:2; $\frac{4}{2}$

3. Suppose that you had $120 in $5 bills and $20 bills. If each group of bills is worth the same amount of money, what is the ratio of $5 bills to $20 bills?

   12 to 3; 12:3; $\frac{12}{3}$

4. Use the information in Problem 3 to find the ratio of $20 bills to all the bills?

   3 to 15; 3:15; $\frac{3}{15}$

5. How is a ratio like a fraction? How is it different?

   Possible answer: A fraction compares parts to a whole, and a ratio can compare parts to a whole; a ratio can also compare parts to parts.

Copyright © Houghton Mifflin Company. All rights reserved.

Equivalent Ratios

Show Your Work

1. Theo practiced his trumpet on 16 different days in April. What is the ratio of days that he practiced the trumpet to all the days in April? Write your answer in simplest form.

   8:15

2. The ratio of boys to girls in the school band is 3:5. If there are 15 girls in the band, how many boys are in the band?

   9 boys

3. Mei Hua performs recitals 2 days out of every 12 days. What is the ratio of days she performs to days she does not perform? Write your answer in simplest form.

   1:5

4. Adam says that the ratio of 18 to 27 in simplest form is 3 to 5. Explain what Adam's mistake was. Then tell the correct answer.

   Adam should have divided 18 and 27 by 9, their GCF; $\frac{18}{27} = \frac{2}{3}$

5. How many whole number ratios equal to 24:30 can you find using division with a whole number divisor? Explain your answer.

   3; *Possible explanation:* the common factors of 24 and 30 are 2, 3, and 6, so the equivalent ratios are 12:15, 8:10, and 4:5.

Copyright © Houghton Mifflin Company. All rights reserved.

Use with text pages 486–487.

Name _____ Date _____

Rates

Show Your Work

1. The Carmel School athletics department spent $756 on sneakers for the boys' and girls' basketball teams. There are 12 players on each team. What was the unit price per pair of sneakers?

   $31.50

2. Liz bought 3 Carmel school sweatshirts. The sweatshirts cost a total of $47.70. What was the unit price per sweatshirt?

   $15.90 per sweatshirt

3. The girls' basketball team has an away game at Salem. The bus travels 40 miles per hour during the half-hour trip. How far apart are the schools?

   20 miles

4. Suppose that a car travels 78 miles in $1\frac{1}{2}$ hours. How can you find the car's speed in miles per hour? Set up equivalent ratios: 78 miles/ 1.5 hours = ? Miles/1 hour, 1.5 ÷ 1.5 = 1 and 78 ÷ 1.5 = 52. The car's speed is 52 mph.

5. Ms. Wilson, the girls' basketball coach, wants to purchase 24 basketballs. She can buy them at a rate of $136 for 4 basketballs or $404 for 12 basketballs. Which is the better buy? Explain.

   $404 for 12 basketballs; Possible explanation: $136 for 4 basketballs is the same as $34 for one basketball, and $404 for 12 basketballs is the same as $33.67 for one basketball.

Copyright © Houghton Mifflin Company. All rights reserved.

Use with text pages 488–490.

Proportions

Show Your Work

1. The Bloomingdale girl scout troop went camping. The troop leader asked 5 girls when they wanted to go hiking. Three of the 5 girls wanted to go hiking in the morning. If there were 25 girls on the trip, how many do you think wanted to go hiking in the morning?

   15 wanted to go hiking in the morning.

2. 18 of 30 scouts who went to the uniform store preferred the new uniforms over the old ones. Suppose that 300 scouts go to the uniform store. Predict how many scouts would prefer the old uniforms.

   120 scouts

3. To make 2 gallons of fruit punch, 2 quarts of concentrated fruit juice are combined with 6 quarts of water. To make 11 gallons of fruit punch, how many quarts of concentrated fruit juice and water are needed?

   11 quarts of concentrated fruit juice and 33 quarts of water

4. Three of every 8 scouts were able to lead a day hike. If 21 scouts were able to lead a day hike, how many scouts were hiking?

   56 scouts

5. Possible answer: Amy did not find cross products: She multiplied 5 by 60 and divided the product, 300, by 12; z = 144.

5. For the proportion $\frac{5}{12} = \frac{60}{z}$, Amy wrote that $z = 25$. Explain what Amy's mistake was. Then tell the correct answer.

Copyright © Houghton Mifflin Company. All rights reserved.

Use with text pages 492–494.

Name _____ Date _____

Similar Figures and Scale Drawings

Show Your Work

1. What value of *x* is needed to make the figures similar?

5 cm [ ] 7 cm

10 cm [ ] *x*

14 cm

_____

2. On a map of a campground, the distance between the general store and the high-way is 5 centimeters. If 1 cm = 500 m on the map, what is the actual distance in kilometers between the general store and the highway?

2.5 km

_____

3. The actual distance between the general store and the lake is 4 kilometers. Use the scale from Problem 2 to find the distance between the general store and the lake on the map.

8 cm

_____

4. Draw 2 different figures that are similar to the figure shown.

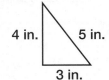

4 in.   5 in.

3 in.

Possible answer: 6 in.
-8 in.-10 in. right triangle
and 9 in.-12 in.-15 in.
right triangle

Check drawings.

_____

5. Which type of triangle is always similar? Explain.

Equilateral triangles.
Possible explanation: Equilateral triangles are always similar to other equilateral triangles because they always have the same shape. All equilateral triangles have three 60° angles.

_____

Copyright © Houghton Mifflin Company. All rights reserved.

Use with text pages 496–498.

Problem-Solving Decision:
Estimate or Exact Answer?

1. At Minnie's Dollhouse Store, a package of 6 pieces of miniature furniture sells for
$27.50. At Dollhouses Etc., a package of 8 pieces of miniature furniture sells for $40.24.
Which is the better buy? Tell whether you used an estimate or an exact answer.

UNDERSTAND

What is the question?

Which dollhouse is the better buy?

What do you know?

Minnie's sells 6 pieces for $27.50
and Dollhouses Etc. sells 8 pieces for $40.24.

PLAN

What can you do to compare the prices
without finding an exact answer?

Estimate the cost per
piece. If too close, find the exact answer.

SOLVE

Did you use an estimate or did you find
the exact answer?

Estimate since
$27.50 ÷ 6 is between $4 and $5 per
piece; $40.24 ÷ 8 > $5
per piece.

Which store offers the better buy?

Minnie's offer is the better buy.

LOOK BACK

Is your answer reasonable? Six pieces at $5 would be
$30, and since $27.50 < $30, the answer
is reasonable.

**Determine whether you need an estimate or an exact answer to solve the
following question.**

2. Tyrone needs to buy pencils for school. He can buy 12 pencils for $3.00 or 20 pencils
for $4.60. Which should Tyrone buy? Tell whether you used an estimate or an
exact answer.

$3.00 ÷ 12 = $0.25 per pencil, $4.60 ÷ 20 =
$0.23 per pencil, so 20 for $4.60 is the better
buy. I needed to find the exact answer.

Copyright © Houghton Mifflin Company. All rights reserved.   **Use with text pages 500–501.**

Name _____ Date _____

Understand Percent

Show Your Work

1. A 10 × 10 grid has 37% of the squares
   shaded. How many of the squares are
   shaded?

   _____37 squares_____

2. In the election for class president,
   Daphne received 40% of the votes,
   Felicia received 35% of the votes, and
   Chet received the rest of the votes. What
   percent did Chet receive? Draw the
   results on a 10 × 10 grid. Color each
   person's percent a different color.

   _____25%; *Check drawings.*_____

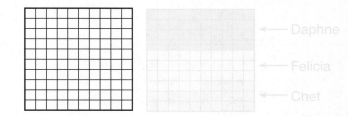

3. Betty said that 84% written as a ratio in
   simplest form is $\frac{42}{50}$. Explain what Betty's
   mistake was. Then tell the correct answer.

   Betty did not divide
   by the greatest common factor; $\frac{21}{25}$

4. What percent of a meter is a centimeter?
   Explain your answer.

   1%; *Possible answer:* There are 100
   centimeters in one meter, so 1 centimeter
   would be 1%.

Copyright © Houghton Mifflin Company. All rights reserved.   **Use with text pages 506–507.**

Relate Fractions, Decimals, and Percents

Show Your Work

1. The Houston Comets had the second-best record in the WNBA during the 2002 season. The Comets won 24 of their 32 games. What percent of their games did the Comets win?

   _____75%_____

2. WNBA teams play 32 games in a regular season. If a WNBA team wins 50% of their games, how many games would they win?

   _____16 games_____

3. How many games would a WNBA team have to win in order to win 25% of the games in a regular season?

   _____8 games_____

4. Suppose that a basketball player attempted 20 three-point shots and made 5 of them. What percent of her shots did she make? Now write your answer as a decimal.

   _____25%; 0.25_____

5. Explain how to change a percent to a decimal.

   Possible answer: Move the decimal point two places to the left and remove the percent sign.

Copyright © Houghton Mifflin Company. All rights reserved.

Use with text pages 508–509.

Name _____   Date _____

Compare Fractions, Decimals, and Percents

Show Your Work

1. In a survey of favorite ice cream, mint chocolate chip received 22% of the votes. Chocolate received $\frac{1}{4}$ of the votes and vanilla received 0.37 of the votes. Order the flavors from most to least popular.

   vanilla, chocolate, mint chocolate chip

2. Using the information in Problem 1, write the part of the votes that other flavors received as a percent, a decimal, and a fraction in simplest form.

   16%; 0.16; $\frac{4}{25}$

3. Ms. Davis's students were surveyed on their favorite subject. One fifth prefer math, 0.35 prefer social studies, and 45% prefer reading. Order the subjects from least favorite to most favorite.

   math, social studies, reading

4. Bart conducted a music survey among his friends. He reported that 0.42 prefer pop, 22% prefer rock, and $\frac{2}{5}$ prefer country. Explain what's wrong with Bart's results.

   The total is 104%, but it should not be greater than 100%.

5. Is it easier to compare percents than it is fractions? Why or why not?

   Answers will vary.

Copyright © Houghton Mifflin Company. All rights reserved.

Use with text pages 510–512.

Name _____ Date _____

Find 10% of a Number

Show Your Work

1. The bill for dinner was $76. Chuck left a 20% tip. How much was the tip?

   $15.20

2. Carol likes to leave 10% of one night's stay for the cleaning crew at a hotel. If the Highfield Hotel charges $155 per night, how much did Carol leave for the cleaning crew?

   $15.50

3. Deanna said she can find 60% of a number by finding 10% of a number and multiplying by 6. Is Deanna correct? Give an example.

   Deanna is correct; Possible example: to find 60% of 100, first find 10%, which is 10. 10 × 6 = 60, which is 60% of 100.

4. Which is greater, 20% of 40 or 40% of 20? Explain your answer.

   They are equal; 20% of 40 is 8 and 40% of 20 is 8.

5. How could you use mental math to find 15% of a number?

   Possible answer: First find 10% of a number and then find half of that number. Then add the numbers.

Copyright © Houghton Mifflin Company. All rights reserved.

Use with text pages 514–515.

Percent of a Number

Show Your Work

1. In the twentieth century, the Republican Party won 52% of the 25 presidential elections. How many presidential elections did they win?

__13 elections__

2. The Anaheim Angels won the 2002 World Series to give the American League baseball teams victories in 54% of the last 50 World Series. How many World Series did the American League teams lose?

__23 World Series__

3. The summer Olympic Games are held every 4 years. The United States has hosted 16% of the 25 summer games. How many times has the United States hosted?

__4 summer Olympics__

4. Jose said that 35% of 60 is 210. Is Jose correct? Explain.

No; Possible explanation: He made a mistake in place value. 35% of 60 is 21.

5. How could you use ratios to find 70% of 80?

Possible answer: Find $\frac{1}{10}$ of 80 (8) and multiply by 7 (8 × 7 = 56).

Copyright © Houghton Mifflin Company. All rights reserved.

Use with text pages 516–518.

Name _____ Date _____

Problem-Solving Application:
Use Circle Graphs

1. How many more students named as their top hero an entertainer than a parent?

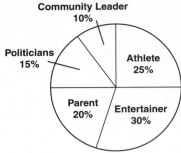

Person Named As Top Hero

Community Leader
10%

Politicians
15%

Athlete
25%

Parent
20%

Entertainer
30%

120 People Surveyed

UNDERSTAND

See circle graph above.

What important information do you know?   120 were surveyed.
20%, parent; 25%, athlete; 15%, politician;
30%, entertainer; and 10%, community leader.

PLAN

Which operation do you need to use to find how many students chose an entertainer?   multiplication

Which operation do you need to use to find how many more one is than another?   subtraction

SOLVE

How many students chose an entertainer?   120 × 30% = 120 × 0.3 = 36

How many students chose a parent?   120 × 20% = 120 × 0.2 = 24

How many more students chose an entertainer than a parent?   12 more students

LOOK BACK

How many students did not choose an entertainer or a parent? Is your answer reasonable?

60; The answer is reasonable since
$\frac{1}{2}$; 120 × $\frac{1}{2}$ = 60.

30% + 20% = 50% or

Draw a circle graph to help you solve.

2. Suppose Sidney got 48 votes and Bessie got 32 votes for class president. How can you show the data as percents in a circle graph?

Sidney got $\frac{48}{80}$ or $\frac{3}{5}$ or 60% of the
votes. Bessie got $\frac{32}{80}$ or $\frac{2}{5}$ or 40% of the votes.
Circle graphs will vary.

Copyright © Houghton Mifflin Company. All rights reserved.

Name _____ Date _____

Make Choices

Show Your Work

1. Hunan Express offers 3 types of soup and 8 main courses. How many choices are there if you want to order a soup and a main course?

   <u>   24 choices   </u>

2. Suppose that Hunan Express also offers 5 drinks. How many choices are there if you want to order a soup, a main course, and a drink?

   <u>   120 choices   </u>

3. Antarctic Ice Cream makes blend-ins, a combination of ice cream and candy. If there are 9 ice cream flavors and 7 candies, how many choices are there if you pick an ice cream flavor and a candy?

   <u>   63 choices   </u>

4. Enzo's Pizzeria offers a lunch special. A customer can order a slice of pizza with a choice of one of 8 toppings and one of 4 desserts. How many possible choices are there for the lunch special?

   <u>   32 choices   </u>

5. Enzo's Pizzeria changed the lunch special so that a customer can now order a slice of pizza with a choice of 8 toppings or a plain calzone and one of 4 desserts. To find the new number of possible choices, should you add 1 to your solution to Problem 3? Explain.

   No; *Possible answer:* To find the number of new choices, multiply: $9 \times 4 = 36$.

Copyright © Houghton Mifflin Company. All rights reserved.

Use with text pages 528–529.

Probability Concepts

Use the following information to solve Problems 1–5.

A shuffle button on a CD player plays songs at random.
Lance has 6 CDs in his CD player. Lance has 3 Generic
Rock CDs, 2 Mr. Rap CDs and 1 Country Clemmons CD.

Show Your Work

1. If Lance presses the shuffle button, is he
   more likely to hear a Generic Rock song
   or a Country Clemmons song?

   __Generic Rock_____

2. If Lance presses the shuffle button, is he
   less likely to hear a Country Clemmons
   song or a Mr. Rap song?

   __Country Clemmons_____

3. To be certain that he will hear a Generic
   Rock song, what 6 CDs should Lance put
   in the CD player?   Lance should put 6 Generic
   Rock CDs in the CD player.

4. Lance's sister, Laura, wants to listen to the
   CDs, but she does not want to hear any of
   Country Clemmons music. Lance said that
   it was impossible for her to hear a Country
   Clemmons song. Is he correct? Explain.   No; *Possible answer:*
   It is less likely that a
   country song will come
   on, but it is not impossible.

5. If Lance presses the shuffle button, is he
   more likely to hear a Country Clemmons
   song or a Razamatazz Jazz song? Explain.   Country Clemmons;
   Possible answer: It is
   impossible for him to hear a Razamatazz Jazz
   song because there are no Razamatazz Jazz
   CDs in the CD player.

Copyright © Houghton Mifflin Company. All rights reserved.

Use with text pages 530–531.

Theoretical Probability

Ms. Forman put the names of her
students into a hat. She is going to
pick names at random for a game.
Use this information to solve
Problems 1–5.

Ms. Forman's Class			
Lisa	Cathy	Marco	Mary
Mark	Dawn	Sue	Barry
Hector	Alyssa	Doug	Christopher
Gautam	Alison	Haruo	John
Brendan	Kim	Sherrie	Donna

Show Your Work

**Express the probability of each event
as a fraction in simplest form.**

1. What is the probability that Ms. Forman
   will pick a name that begins with a
   vowel?

   $\frac{1}{10}$

   _____

2. What is the probability that the name
   picked will not begin with a *D*?

   $\frac{17}{20}$

   _____

3. What is the probability that the name
   picked will begin with an *A*, *B*, or *C*?

   $\frac{3}{10}$

   _____

4. Use the data in the chart to write a
   problem about the probability of picking
   a name. Then solve it.

   Answers will vary.

   _____

5. Donna said that the probability of Ms.
   Forman picking a name that begins with
   T was 0. Is she correct? Explain.

   Yes; Possible answer:
   There are no names that
   begin with *T*, so the outcome is impossible
   and the probability is 0.

Copyright © Houghton Mifflin Company. All rights reserved.

Use with text pages 532–534.

Problem-Solving Strategy:
Make an Organized List

1. Renee, Jessica, and Anjali are competing in the finals of the obstacle course. How many different ways can they finish?

UNDERSTAND

What is the question asking you to find?

How many different ways can Renee, Jessica, and Anjali finish the obstacle course?

What do you know?

3 girls are competing in the obstacle course. They can each come in first, second, or third.

PLAN

Make an organized list to show all the possible ways that the competitors can finish.

R-J-A, R-A-J, J-A-R, J-R-A, A-J-R, A-R-J

SOLVE

How many possibilities are there for Renee to win? For Jessica to win? For Anjali? How many different ways can they finish?

2; 2; 2; 6

LOOK BACK

Does your solution make sense?

Yes; each girl can finish in first 2 different ways, second 2 different ways, and third 2 different ways.

Make an organized list to solve the following problem.

2. Beth, Andrea, Nancy, Tanya, Christine, and Helene all want to be the starters on the basketball team. Five of them can start. How many different combinations of starters can be chosen from this group?

6; Possible answer: Each girl has 5 chances to start and 1 not to start, so the solution makes sense.

Copyright © Houghton Mifflin Company. All rights reserved.

Use with text pages 536–538.

Experimental Probability

Show Your Work

1. What is the theoretical probability of rolling a number cube labeled 1–6 and getting a 4? Complete 30 rolls and record your results. How many times did you roll a 4?

   $\frac{1}{6}$; 5 times

2. What is the theoretical probability of rolling a number cube labeled 1–6 and getting an even number? Complete 20 rolls and record your results. How many times did you roll an even number?

   $\frac{1}{2}$; 10 times

3. What is the theoretical probability of tossing a coin and getting heads? Complete 20 tosses and record your results. How many times did you toss heads?

   $\frac{1}{2}$; 10 times

1–3: Results of experiments will vary. Theoretical probabilities and sample predictions are given.

4. A red and blue spinner is spun 40 times. The spinner landed on red 30 times and on blue 10 times. Draw what you think the spinner should look like. Explain your drawing.

   $\frac{30}{40}$ is the same as $\frac{3}{4}$ and $\frac{10}{40}$ is the same as $\frac{1}{4}$.

   Blue
   Red

5. If you roll a number cube labeled 1–6 50 times, would you expect to get each number the same number of times? Explain why or why not.

   No; Possible answer: There are 6 possible outcomes and $50 \div 6 = 8$ R2. Since there is a remainder, it is impossible for the numbers to be rolled the same number of times.

Copyright © Houghton Mifflin Company. All rights reserved.

Use with text pages 540–542.

Name _____   Date _____

Compound Events

Show Your Work

1. Suppose that you play a game in which you roll a number cube labeled 1–6 and toss a penny. What is the probability of getting a number greater than 2 and heads?

   _____ $\frac{1}{3}$ _____

2. Make an organized list of all the possible outcomes of flipping two coins.

   _____ H-H, H-T, T-H, T-T _____

3. Use your solution to Problem 2 to find the probability of both coins landing on heads.

   _____ $\frac{1}{4}$ _____

4. Suppose that you roll two number cubes, each of which is labeled 1–6. What is the probability of rolling a 3 with the first number cube and a 5 with the second number cube?

   _____ $\frac{1}{36}$ _____

5. Describe a compound event where the probability for both events to occur is $\frac{1}{8}$. *Possible answer:* I can spin a spinner with 4 equal parts, numbered 1, 2, 3, and 4, and toss a coin. Each of the 8 combinations will have a probability of $\frac{1}{8}$.

Copyright © Houghton Mifflin Company. All rights reserved.

Use with text pages 544–545.

Problem-Solving Application:
Make Predictions

1. Mr. Grady's class was asked to choose the school nickname.
If 10 of the 25 students chose Tigers, how many of the
400 students at Taylor School would you expect to say Tigers?

UNDERSTAND

What is the question?

How many of the 400 students at Taylor would vote for Tigers as a school nickname?

_____

What do you know?

I know that 10 of 25 students in Mr. Grady's class voted for Tigers.

_____

PLAN

What is the formula for probability?

$$\frac{\text{number of favorable outcomes}}{\text{number of possible outcomes}}$$

_____

SOLVE

Which operation do you need to use to predict the
number of students at Taylor who would vote Tigers?

multiplication

_____

Find the number of students who would
say Tigers.

$$\frac{10}{25} = \frac{x}{400}, \; x = 160$$

_____

LOOK BACK

Is the answer reasonable?

$$\frac{160}{400} = \frac{2}{5} = \frac{10}{25},$$ so the answer is reasonable.

_____

Solve the following problem by using data to make predictions.

2. If 6 students in Mr. Grady's class said Patriots,
how many of the 400 students at Taylor School
could be expected to say Patriots or Tigers?

The probability is $\frac{(10 + 6)}{25}$ or $\frac{16}{25}$; $\frac{16}{25} = \frac{x}{400}$; $x = 256$.

_____

Copyright © Houghton Mifflin Company. All rights reserved.

Use with text pages 546–548.

Model Equations

Show Your Work

1. In $c + 5 = 9$, what value does c represent?

$\underline{c = 4}$

2. Multiply both sides of the equation in Problem 1 by 3. What value does c represent now?

$\underline{c = 4}$

3. In $24 \div x = 8$, what value does x represent?

$\underline{x = 3}$

4. Divide both sides of the equation in Problem 3 by 2. What value does x represent now?

$\underline{x = 3}$

5. If you add 25 to both sides of the equation in Problem 3, will the value of x change? Explain your answer.

No; Possible explanation: As long as the operations are done exactly the same to both sides, the value of x will not change.

Copyright © Houghton Mifflin Company. All rights reserved.

Use with text pages 566–567.

Write and Solve Equations

Write and solve an equation for each problem.

Show Your Work

1. Rosie had $20 before she went to the movies. After the movies she had $7. How much did she spend at the movies?

   $$\$20 = x + \$7;\ x = \$13$$

2. Rosie's father had $17 in his wallet. He went to an ATM to take out money. After the ATM withdrawal he had $67. How much money did he take out?

   $$17 + x = 67;\ x = 50;\ \$50$$

3. Lianna treated 3 of her friends and herself to ice cream sundaes. The bill for the sundaes was $16. Each sundae cost the same amount. How much was each sundae?

   $$16 = 4x;\ x = 4;\ \$4$$

4. Claudia has 147 CDs. She stores the CDs on 7 shelves, and each shelf has the same number of CDs. How many CDs are on each shelf?

   $$147 = 7x;\ x = 21;\ 21 \text{ CDs on each shelf}$$

5. For $6z = 126$, Mike wrote that $z = 756$. Explain what Mike's mistake was. Then tell the correct answer.

   Possible explanation: Mike multiplied one side by 6 instead of dividing both sides by 6; $z = 21$.

Copyright © Houghton Mifflin Company. All rights reserved.

Use with text pages 568–570.

Name _____   Date _____

Problem-Solving Strategy:
Write an Equation

1. Mr. Martinez owns his own business. As a salary, he earns $2\frac{1}{2}$ times as much as Juan. Mr. Martinez makes $2,000 each week. How much is Juan paid per week?

UNDERSTAND

Mr. Martinez earns $2,000 each week;
he makes $2\frac{1}{2}$ times
Juan's salary.

What information do you know?

_____

What do you need to find out?

How much Juan gets paid.

PLAN

Which operation can you use to find out how much Juan is paid? __division__

SOLVE

Let *j* represent Juan. What equation can you write to solve the problem?

$2\frac{1}{2}j = 2,000, j = 800$

How much is Juan paid?

$800 per week.

LOOK BACK

How can you check your answer?

$800 \times 2\frac{1}{2} = 2,000$

Write an equation to solve the following problem.

2. In the last four weeks, Yow worked 150 hours. If she worked $\frac{1}{3}$ of the hours last week, how many hours did she work the previous three weeks? Explain your answer.

$\frac{1}{3} \cdot 150 = x; x = 50$ hours; $150 - 50 = 100$ hours; 100 hours the previous 3 weeks

Copyright © Houghton Mifflin Company. All rights reserved.

Use with text pages 572–574.

Variables and Functions

Show Your Work

1. Tracey's pay is described by the rule
$y = 8x$, where y represents the amount
of pay in dollars and x represents the
number of hours she worked. How much
money does Tracey earn if she works
6 hours?

   $48

2. Use the function rule from Problem 1.
How much money does Tracey earn if
she works 8 hours?

   $64

3. Use the function rule from Problem 1. If
Tracey earned $72, how many hours did
she work? If she earned $88, how many
hours did she work?

   9 hours; 11 hours

4. Make a function table to show how the
number of cups is related to the number
of pints. The relationship between cups
(x) and pints (y) can be described by the
rule $y = \frac{1}{2}x$. Give 5 values of x.

   Check function tables.
   Possible answer:

x	y
2	1
4	2
6	3
8	4
10	5

5. Explain how making a function table can
help you to solve problems.

   Possible answer: It shows the relationship
   between two variables when the relationship
   stays the same.

Copyright © Houghton Mifflin Company. All rights reserved.

Use with text pages 576–577.

Patterns and Functions

**Use the information below for Problems 1–5. When Lenny exercises,
it takes him 20 minutes to warm up and 8 minutes to run one mile.**

Show Your Work

1. Write an equation that relates the total
amount of time Lenny exercises (y) to
the amount of warm-up time and the
number of miles he runs (x).

   Possible answer: $y = 20 + 8x$

2. For how many minutes will Lenny
exercise if he runs 4 miles?

   52 minutes

3. For how many minutes will Lenny
exercise if he runs 7.5 miles?

   80 minutes

4. If Lenny exercised for an hour, how
many miles did he run?

   5 miles

5. Lenny exercised for 2 hours and said he
ran 10 miles. Explain Lenny's mistake.
Then tell the correct answer.

   Possible answer: Lenny
doubled the number of
miles he ran in one hour instead of solving the
equation. The correct answer is $12\frac{1}{2}$ miles.

Copyright © Houghton Mifflin Company. All rights reserved.

Use with text pages 578–581.

Name _____ Date _____

Integers and Absolute Value

Show Your Work

1. The lowest temperature ever recorded
   in Alaska was 80 degrees Fahrenheit
   below zero. Write that temperature as
   an integer.

   _____$-80°F$_____

2. The lowest temperature ever recorded
   in Hawaii was 12 degrees Fahrenheit.
   What is the opposite of that temperature
   written as an integer?

   _____$-12°F$_____

3. A quarterback is sacked for a loss of
   8 yards. Write that distance as an
   integer. What is its opposite?

   _____-8 yards; 8 yards_____

4. Professional golfers try to score under
   par. Draw a number line to show a
   golfer with a score of -4 and another
   with a score of $+3$.

   _____

5. Is $+2$ greater than all the negative
   integers? Explain.

   Yes; *Possible explanation:* $+2$ is to the
   right of 0 on a number line, and all the
   negative integers are to the left of 0. The
   farther a number is to the right of 0, the
   greater the number.

Copyright © Houghton Mifflin Company. All rights reserved.

Use with text pages 586–587.

Compare and Order Integers

Show Your Work

1. At the 2002 U.S. Women's Golf Open, the top three finishers had the following scores: $^-4$, $^+3$, $^-2$. The least score wins. Place the golfers' scores in order from best to worst.

   _____ $^-4$, $^-2$, $^+3$ _____

2. Write three scores that are better than the worst score in Problem 1 but not as good as the middle score in Problem 1.

   Possible answer: $^+2$, $^+1$, 0

3. Sarah ordered these integers from least to greatest: 2, $^-3$, 4, $^-5$. Explain what Sarah's mistake was. Then tell the correct answer. Sarah ordered the absolute values from least to greatest. The correct order from least to greatest is $^-5$, $^-3$, 2, 4.

4. Write a mixed number, a decimal, and an improper fraction that are between $^-1$ and $^-2$.

   Possible answer: $^-1\frac{1}{2}$, $^-1.2$, $^-\frac{4}{3}$

5. Are all negative rational numbers less than all positive rational numbers? Explain. Yes; Possible explanation: The negative rational numbers are all to the left of 0 on a number line and the positive rational numbers are all to the right of 0. The farther a number is to the right of 0, the greater the number.

Copyright © Houghton Mifflin Company. All rights reserved.

Use with text pages 588–590.

Model Addition of Integers

Use the data from the chart to solve Problems 1–4.

Golf Scoring						
Name	Eagle	Birdie	Par	Bogey	Double Bogey	Triple Bogey
Score	⁻2	⁻1	0	⁺1	⁺2	⁺3

Show Your Work

1. Through 6 holes Alexia has a score of ⁻2. On the seventh hole she gets a birdie. What is Alexia's score now?

   ___⁻3___

2. Using three different scores, how could a golfer get a score of ⁺1?

   Possible answer: double bogey, birdie, par

3. Bobby had a score of ⁻1 until he got an eagle. He said his score is now ⁺1. Explain what Bobby's mistake was. Then tell the correct answer.

   Possible answer: Bobby added ⁺2 to his score, not ⁻2; His score is ⁻3.

4. What score would someone have if they got birdie, par, birdie, and eagle?

   ___⁻4___

5. When is the sum of a positive integer and a negative integer 0? Give an example.

   Possible answer: If the positive integer and negative integer have the same absolute value, the sum will be 0; for example, ⁻2 + ⁺2 = 0.

Copyright © Houghton Mifflin Company. All rights reserved.

Use with text pages 592–594.

Name _____ Date _____

Model Subtraction of Integers

Show Your Work

1. What is the difference when you subtract $^+3$ from $^+2$?

   <u>$^-1$</u>

2. What is $^-5 - {}^-3$?

   <u>$^-2$</u>

3. Eileen wrote that $^-4 - {}^+4 = 0$. Explain what Eileen's mistake was. Then tell the correct answer.

   <u>Eileen added 4 instead of subtracting 4; $^-8$</u>

4. The sum of two integers is $^-3$. The difference of the same two integers is $^-13$. What are the integers?

   <u>$^-8$ and $^+5$</u>

5. If a negative integer is subtracted from a positive integer, can the answer be 0? Explain and give an example.

   <u>No; Possible answer: The difference between a positive integer and a negative integer will result in a greater positive integer: for example, $4 - {}^-3$ is the same as $4 + 3 = 7$.</u>

Copyright © Houghton Mifflin Company. All rights reserved.

Use with text pages 596–597.

Add and Subtract Integers

Show Your Work

1. In 2001, the lowest temperature in Anchorage, Alaska, was ⁻15°F. The lowest temperature in Fairbanks, Alaska, was ⁻41°F. How many degrees colder was the lowest temperature in Fairbanks?

   _____ 26°F _____

2. The lowest temperature in Chicago, Illinois, was ⁻27°F. The lowest temperature in Portland, Maine, was 12° colder. What was the lowest temperature in Portland?

   _____ ⁻39°F _____

3. The lowest temperature ever recorded in Florida was ⁻2°F. If you subtract 38°, you will find the lowest temperature ever recorded in Arizona. What is that temperature?

   _____ ⁻40°F _____

4. The lowest temperature in Bismarck, North Dakota, was ⁻44°F. If you subtract ⁻153°, you will find Bismarck's highest temperature. What is that temperature?

   _____ 109°F _____

5. Can you subtract two positive numbers and get a negative number? Explain and give an example.

   Yes; Possible explanation: When the number being subtracted is greater than the number it is being subtracted from, the difference will be negative: for example, 4 − 5 = ⁻1.

Copyright © Houghton Mifflin Company. All rights reserved.

Use with text pages 598–600.

Problem-Solving Application:
Use Integers

1. The wind chill temperature at 9 A.M. is ⁻22 degrees Fahrenheit. The wind chill temperature is 27 degrees colder than the actual temperature. What is the actual temperature?

UNDERSTAND

What does the question ask? What is the actual temperature if it is 27 degrees warmer than ⁻22?

PLAN

What does ⁻22 degrees mean? 22° less than 0

Is the wind chill temperature greater or less than the actual temperature?
less

SOLVE

What number sentence can you write to find the actual temperature?
⁻22 + 27 = actual temperature

What is the actual temperature?
5°F

LOOK BACK

How can you check your answer?
5 − 27 = ⁻22

Solve.

2. The temperature outside is 6 degrees Fahrenheit at 6 P.M. By midnight the temperature drops 9 degrees and by 3 A.M. it drops another 5 degrees. What is the temperature at 3 A.M.?

⁻8°F

Copyright © Houghton Mifflin Company. All rights reserved.

Use with text pages 602–604.

Integers and the Coordinate Plane

Use grid paper to help you solve Problems 1–5.

Show Your Work

1. Starting from the origin, what movements do you need to plot the ordered pair ($^+$3, $^-$4)? In which quadrant is this ordered pair located?

   Move right to $^+$3, and down to $^-$4; Quadrant IV.

2. Start at ($^+$3, $^-$4). If you go to the left 4 places and up 2 places, what are the coordinates of the new ordered pair?

   ($^-$1, $^-$2)

3. Draw a pentagon on grid paper. List the ordered pairs.

   Check drawings.

4. If $x = 2$ and $y = 3$, find the coordinates for the ordered pair ($x - 3$, $y + 2$).

   ($^-$1, $^+$5)

5. India plotted the ordered pairs ($^+$1, $^+$3), ($^+$3, $^+$3), and ($^+$3, $^+$1). She connected the points and said she made a square. Explain what India's mistake was. How could she correct her mistake?

   India made a right triangle, not a square. To correct her mistake, she needs to plot another point, (1, 1), and connect the four points.

Copyright © Houghton Mifflin Company. All rights reserved.

Use with text pages 610–612.

Integers and Functions

1. The function $g = s + 30$ expresses Gloria's age (g) in terms of Stephanie's age (s). How old will Gloria be when Stephanie is 33?

   _____ 63 _____

2. Use the function from Problem 1. How old will Stephanie be when Gloria is 75?

   _____ 45 _____

3. The function $y = 2x - 1$ describes the path a storm is taking. At noon, $x = 0$. Find the value of y at noon.

   _____ $y = {}^-1$ _____

4. Use the function from Problem 3 to find the value of y when $x = 1, 2,$ or 3.

   _____ $y = 1, 3, 5$ _____

5. Explain the steps you used to solve Problem 2.

   _____ Possible answer: I substituted 75 for g to get $75 = s + 30$. I then subtracted 30 from both sides of the equation to get $45 = s$.

Copyright © Houghton Mifflin Company. All rights reserved.

Use with text pages 614–615.

Name _____ Date _____

Use Functions and Graphs

Show Your Work

1. Find values of y to complete the function table.

$y = x + 2$	
x	y
4	6
6	8
8	10

2. Graph the function in Problem 1 on grid paper.

3. Find values of y to complete the function table. Then graph the function on grid paper.

$y = 4x - 3$	
x	y
0	-3
1	1
2	5
3	9

4. Find 5 ordered pairs for the function $y = x - 5$. Then graph the function on grid paper.

Possible answer:

$y = x - 5$	
x	y
-2	-7
-1	-6
0	-5
1	-4
2	-3

5. A hurricane travels along a path described by the function $y = 3x - 2$. The town of Kingston lies at (4, 10). Is Kingston in the path of the hurricane? Explain your answer.

Yes; Possible answer: substitute 4 for x to get $y = 4 \times 3 - 2$, $y = 12 - 2 = 10$, so Kingston is in the path of the hurricane.

Copyright © Houghton Mifflin Company. All rights reserved.

Use with text pages 616–618.

Problem-Solving Application:
Use a Graph

1. This graph shows how much it costs for a dog to stay at the Doggie Hotel kennel for several days. What would it cost the Lennox family if their dog stays at the Doggie Hotel for a week?

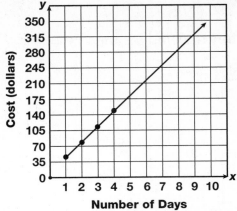

UNDERSTAND

What is the question? How much would it cost the Lennox family if their dog stays at the Doggie Hotel for a week?

What do you know? The Lennox family is going away for a week. It costs $40 for 1 day, $75 for 2 days, $110 for 3 days, and $145 for 4 days.

PLAN

Do you see a pattern?
The price goes up $35 dollars each day.

Let *x* represent the number of days and *y* represent the total cost in dollars. What is the function shown in the graph?
The function is $y = 35x + 5$.

SOLVE

Extend the graph. How much would it cost to kennel the dog for 5 days? 6 days? 7 days?
$180; $215; $250. It cost the Lennox family $250 to board their dog for a week.

LOOK BACK

How can you check that your answer is reasonable?
$35 × 7 + $5 = $250

Use a graph to help solve the following problem.

2. Six months from now, the Lennox family is planning a 2-week vacation. Canine Quarters offers a 2-week rate of $500. Is this a better deal than Doggie Hotel? Explain your answer.
No; The Doggie Hotel is $5 cheaper than Canine Quarters. The Doggie Hotel is $495, which is $5 cheaper than 2 weeks at Canine Quarters.

Copyright © Houghton Mifflin Company. All rights reserved.

Use with text pages 620–621.

Name _____ Date _____

Transformations in the Coordinate Plane

Use grid paper to graph the figures and solve Problems 1–3.

Show Your Work

1. Square *ABCD* has the following coordinates: (2, 3), (2, 7), (6, 3), and (6, 7). It is
   translated right 4 units and up 2 units.
   What are the square's coordinates after
   the translation?

   (6, 5), (6, 9), (10, 5), (10, 9)

2. Triangle *EFG* starts at (⁻4, ⁺5), (⁻4, ⁺1),
   and (⁻1, ⁺1). The triangle is reflected
   across the *y*-axis. What are its new
   coordinates?

   (4, 5), (4, 1), (1, 1)

3. Triangle *HIJ* starts at (4, 6), (1, 2), and
   (4, 2). Rotate it 270° about (0, 0). What
   are its new coordinates?

   (⁻2, 1), (⁻2, 4), (⁻6, 4)

4. If a figure is rotated 360°, what will it
   look like?

   It will be in its original position.

5. Is a figure that has been reflected,
   rotated, or translated congruent to its
   original figure? Explain.

   Yes; Possible answer:
   a transformed figure
   only changes loca-
   tion. Its shape and
   size remain intact.

Copyright © Houghton Mifflin Company. All rights reserved. **Use with text pages 622–624.**